The ABCs

of

LAW SCHOOL

The ABCs
of
LAW SCHOOL

DIARY OF A FIRST YEAR STUDENT

TERESA POWER, JD

STAFFORD·HOUSE·BOOKS

For information, address Stafford House Books, Inc.
P.O. Box 291, Pacific Palisades, CA 90272
www.staffordhousebooks.com

The author and publisher of this book disclaim any liability in connection with the exercises and advice contained herein.

ISBN: 978-0-9981070-7-3 Paperback
ISBN: 978-0-9981070-8-0 eBook
Library of Congress Control Number: 2018913097

Editing: Cheryle Lynn Reeves and Tracy Grigoriades
Book Design: Dotti Albertine
Yoga illustrations by Ivana Mundja
Printed on acid-free paper

This book is dedicated to Kaitlyn and Emmet,
my amazing children
who are such loving, caring, and talented young adults.
May you both always follow your dreams,
wherever they take you in life!

CONTENTS

PREFACE

Why I Wrote this Book

ARE YOU THINKING of becoming a lawyer? Are you intrepidly facing your first year of law school? Do you feel overwhelmed? Never fear. You're not alone. I've been through it and made it to the other side. I wrote this book to help you do the same.

Ever since I was a young girl, I dreamed of being an attorney, helping others solve their problems and making a difference in the world. But, dreaming of being a lawyer and becoming one are two very different things. I wish that I'd had a guide like this when I cluelessly embarked on my legal adventure. Law school is hard, but it's possible to survive and thrive using the strategies and information shared in this book.

Fast forward past law school, to real life. The year was 1997. After practicing law for several years in the areas of Real Estate and Personal Injury/Insurance Defense, I decided to press pause on my law career and become a stay-at-home mom. I was at a crossroads on my life journey. I wanted to be with my two young children; yet. I still yearned to make a difference in the world and help bright students find their place in the legal profession. I've always loved writing and teaching, so authoring this book was a natural progression.

The timing couldn't have been better. The number of applicants to law schools in the 1997-98 academic year was 73,500, marking the first increase in applications since 1991. So, why did I wait until now to publish it? More importantly, is it still relevant?

This diary is just as relevant today as when I wrote it. Just like in 1997, we're currently seeing an interesting trend of increased law school applications, a reversal of the low demand over the past several years. The world will always need lawyers, so it's a perfect time to start your journey.

While some years have passed since I was in law school, the structure by which the legal system works is essentially unchanged, and understanding it starts with your first year of law school. Through research with current law professors and students, I updated this book where necessary to bring it current with the way things are done today. This diary is written from the perspective of how I was taught during my first year, and I have noted accordingly where this differs from today's first year law experience. The essence of what is taught during the first year of law school is basically the same as it was when I was a student at Pepperdine University in Malibu in the 1980s, with some curriculum tweaks which I will discuss in Chapter 3.

There is a trend toward consolidation of classes during the first year, but the subject matter of these core courses is more or less the same from school to school. The actual class organization may be a bit fluid, changing format from year to year as law schools seek to find the best way to present the curriculum. Law school, as well as the actual practice of law itself, is and will always be characterized by substantial amounts of reading, writing and researching. You will become immersed in the Black Letter Law, which is essentially unchanging over time.

Black Letter Law is well-established case law. It describes the fundamental principles of law that are accepted by a majority of judges in most states. The way the law is taught may vary from law school to law school, but the basic rules remain the same. This book will give you a big picture view of these crucial elements of the law.

It's important to stay up to date with changes in the law school preparation process as well as on the dreaded **bar examination**. This exam is meant to determine whether a candidate is qualified to practice law in a particular state. It is currently a two-day exam, as opposed to three days when I took it.

The **Multistate Bar Examination (MBE)** is administered on the first day of the bar examination and is a standardized 200-item test covering six areas of law studied during law school (**Constitutional Law, Contracts, Criminal Law, Evidence, Real Property**, and **Torts**.) The second day of the bar examination involves essay writing on a broad range of subject matters. In addition, a new trend in a growing number of states is to include two nationally developed tests, the **Multistate Essay Examination** (MEE) and the **Multistate Performance Test** (MPT), on the bar examination.

During my legal journey, I started taking yoga classes to help me unwind from the stress of law school and, eventually, from the practice of law itself. Yoga helped me to relax, focus and concentrate, as well as to sort through my priorities. I still maintain a regular yoga practice today, which helps me keep calm and centered in a world filled with instant gratification and the demands of ever-present technology.

After my children were older, I became a yoga teacher, and eventually an author and publisher of children's yoga books, leaving this project on the back burner. Recently, I unearthed this manuscript and was struck by its value; so, I decided to once again take a leap of faith and change my life direction.

My aspiration is to open your mind to the inner-workings of what the law is all about. This essential guide will not only help you to decipher the process of applying to law school, but also to understand the concepts behind the complex material covered during your first year. Even if you are not thinking of going to law school, this book can help you understand the tricky legal process.

Everyone wants to stand out in law school. By understanding the basic concepts and learning how to study, prepare and participate in classes BEFORE the first day, you will have an edge over your classmates. Now, let the journey begin!

ACKNOWLEDGMENTS

I WOULD FIRST like to thank Professor Barry McDonald, who teaches courses in constitutional law, First Amendment law, comparative constitutional law, intellectual property law, and contracts law, for taking the time to read my original manuscript and for all the valuable feedback he gave to me. Asking a current law professor at Pepperdine to read something I wrote over 20 years ago took an act of faith and courage on my part, and I am so glad that I did! His insights and suggestions gave me the confidence to move forward with the book.

That brings me to the next person I would like to thank who is Cheryle Lynn Reeves, my legal editor. She worked meticulously to make sure that all the legal concepts were up to date, and helped me to format and organize the book into its current state. She is the owner and editor of The Persnickety Word Nerd, and true to the name of her company, Cheryle's attention to detail was flawless.

I would also like to thank Tracy Grigoriades, who also worked tirelessly on the copyediting for this book. She also has a sharp eye for details and gave me a fresh perspective on the manuscript from someone who is not a lawyer.

Next, I would like to thank my children, Kaitlyn and Emmet, who patiently listened to me talk endlessly about this book, and for giving me support and encouragement along the way. I would also like to thank my father, who supported me not only in my legal career, but also as I changed paths to become a yoga teacher and children's book author and publisher.

In addition, my mother not only supported me in my decision to take a year off from law school after my first year, but also 'nudged me' to go back and graduate. She has always encouraged me to follow through on my decisions if they are in my best interest, and I am glad that I listened to her sage advice.

And of course this book could not be possible without the amazing education I received at Pepperdine Law School.

I am very grateful for everyone who has believed in me, and I hope that you enjoy this book as much as I enjoyed writing it!

How to Use this Book to Survive and Thrive in Law School

CONGRATULATIONS ON YOUR decision to go to law school! Or, if you've already been accepted, kudos to you. You studied hard in college, binge-watched every episode of your favorite law-related television shows, and have an idealized picture in your head of what law school will be like. So did I. But nothing in my life or previous schooling had prepared me for the adventure I was to embark upon. I had graduated college Cum Laude with a Bachelor of Arts degree in History. I was a member of *Phi Beta Kappa* and used to getting top grades. Yet, within the first three weeks of starting law school, I received a C on a Legal Research and Writing paper and felt like throwing in the towel.

My first year of law school was definitely a humbling experience. I wasted so much time trying to decipher the lawyering process and translating the specialized legal jargon my professors so freely meted out. But, by my second year, patterns began to emerge as to what my professors were looking for. I learned to study smarter and began to crack the code. Soon, I had received two American Jurisprudence awards, which are given to law school students for achieving the highest grade and rank in the class for a particular subject. My only regret was not knowing what to expect from that first year. But don't worry—this book will show you what *really* goes on behind closed classroom doors so you can start and finish strong.

You hold in your hands a secret weapon to law school success. This book will help you to:

- **Survive,** by understanding the bigger picture of your core classes and how everything is interrelated; and
- **Thrive,** by mastering a sound strategy to both prepare for examinations and participate in your classes.

In addition to scratching the surface of the core subjects taught during law school (**Torts, Legal Research and Writing, Contracts, Civil Procedure, Criminal Law and Procedure, Real Property, Constitutional Law, and Evidence**), we'll also cover:

- Briefing a law case
- Using the IRAC method to analyze a case and to write papers and final exams
- Preparing course outlines (detailed outlines for each class are provided at the end of this book and are available for download at www.abclawschooldiary.com).

INTRODUCTION

The law is immense, with volumes of books and treatises available on each of the subjects covered in this book. Upon starting your education, you do not need a full, in-depth understanding of every nuance, especially since each school follows a different curriculum. Instead, this book will help you to connect the dots in a strategic way from the get-go.

You may want to read (or re-read) the chapter on each course before your first day of that class. By having an overview of the subject matter and how professors generally teach the information, you'll make a better first impression and also have an edge over your classmates. Plus, class will make more sense overall, which better facilitates learning. This guidebook can also be used to refresh your memory of important concepts as you maneuver through school.

Although I started out my legal education in the dark, I definitely made it through that first year in the light. As a bonus, I became very close to my fellow classmates and am still friends with many of them today. A very special bond is forged with those in the trenches with you. Not only did I share a sense of community with my classmates, but also with my professors. Once I got over the fear of being called on in class, I began to take advantage of the individual help offered by the faculty and appreciated the open-door policy at Pepperdine Law School.

My goal in writing this diary is to give you a better understanding of a typical first year law student's experience. Although I have tried to simplify complex ideas that we spent an entire year studying, my coverage of each individual subject is in no way exhaustive. Rather, I hope you will learn from my personal experience and will be better equipped to survive yours. I wish someone would have given me this book when I started law school. It would have saved me a lot of time, stress, and anxiety.

Thirty-four years ago, I embarked on a journey to become a lawyer, and that decision has shaped the direction that my life has taken. I hope that this book will become a trusted tool to help you to survive and thrive in law school by providing you with a firm understanding of the materials, mechanics and tools used to teach each particular subject. As a bonus, I am also including a section on stress management through yoga for law students.

This book is divided into three sections, each corresponding to the **ABCs** of Law School. Section **A** is about applications and admissions; **B** goes behind-the-scenes of your first year; and **C** covers class outlines and survival skills. So, without any further ado, let's move onward and upward to pursuing the noble legal profession, starting with the law school preparation process.

PART I

A is for Applications and Admissions

CHAPTER 1

The Law School Admissions Process

In this chapter...

- ✓ The LSAT
- ✓ The GRE as a basis for admission into law school
- ✓ Registering for CAS

THE "A" PORTION of the *ABCs of Law School* refers to **applications and admissions**. Going to law school is not as simple as just filling out an application and *Voila!* You're accepted! The practice of law is a highly regarded profession and one which has designed its training process with time-honored educational traditions that not only teach one how to become a lawyer, but are actually geared toward bringing the best and brightest students into the profession. So, before one can go to law school, one must first prove one's academic fitness to become a lawyer. That being said, setting your mind to what you want to accomplish is half the battle, as evidenced by this quote by Abraham Lincoln: "If you are absolutely determined to make a lawyer of yourself, the thing is more than half done already."

The LSAT

The Law School Admission Test (LSAT) and one's grade point average (GPA) are the barometers by which law schools judge applicants during the admissions process. My GPA was strong at 3.65 but what about that elusive LSAT score? This test was vastly different from any test I had ever taken. There were no facts to learn and nothing to memorize. Instead, all you do on the LSAT is think. Unfortunately, it is a process often easier said than done.

The LSAT has been in use in one form or another since the 1940s. As with any standardized test, the LSAT is not a perfect measurement tool. However, since 1991, when it was first used in its present format, it has been a consistent and relatively accurate tool in determining the potential of law school applicants. The current test is broken down into five sections:

1. Analytical Reasoning (Logic Games);
2. Reading Comprehension;
3. Logical Reasoning (Arguments, consisting of two sections);
4. An Experimental section; and
5. Writing Sample section (short essay).

You may be asking yourself what the above has to do with your first year of law school. The answer lies in your ability to use reasoning and logic skills to analyze information. As we will see later on, that is what law school, and indeed being an attorney, is all about. Your first year of law school involves reading an inordinate amount of legal cases, learning to discern the issues involved in each case and applying rules of law. The LSAT tests your ability to do this.

The test consists of approximately 101 multiple choice questions, but you will only be graded on the questions you answer correctly. Incorrectly answered questions do not count against your score. The number of correctly answered questions becomes what is termed your "raw score." Raw scores are then converted to an LSAT scale through the calculation of a standard error of measurement. The converted score for the LSAT ranges from 120 to 180.

You will also receive a percentile score which ranks your performance relative to the scores of a sample group of other LSAT participants.

Looking at Table 1.1 on the following page, if your scaled score is 165, you would be in the 75th percentile. The experimental section and the writing sample essay are not graded and do not count against your final LSAT score. Your answers to the experimental questions (which are multiple-choice) will help the Law School Admissions Council (LSAC) determine if the questions are good in determining analytical skills and may eventually be included on future LSATs.

Copies of the writing sample, however, will be sent to all the law schools to which you apply. Writing is heavily weighted on the LSAT and in the legal profession in general. Writing

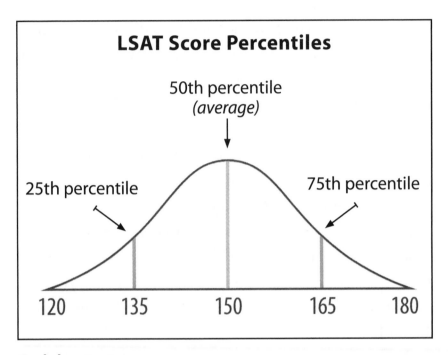

LSAT Score Percentiles

50th percentile
(average)

25th percentile

75th percentile

120   135   150   165   180

Table 1.1

comprises a significant amount of the work attorneys perform on a daily basis and, according to a 2015 LSAT survey of 129 United States and Canadian law schools, almost all of those schools used the sample essay to evaluate the writing ability of applicants. Frivolous essays or failure to write one have been used by law schools as grounds for rejection of applications.

The legal field is extremely competitive. The advice I would give those aspiring to attend law school is to first focus on your college GPA and then the LSAT. If you determine relatively early on in your college career that you wish to go to law school, you can choose courses designed to function as a sort of "pre-law" curriculum, in much the same way many students destined for medical school prepare for their medical training through a pre-med curriculum that is heavily science-based. For example, many students headed toward a career goal of criminal law may wish to take courses in criminal justice. However, since the legal world has many disciplines, focusing on a specific area of undergraduate study is in many ways unnecessary.

Law students enter law school each year with degrees of all kinds, and with the number of laws being enacted every year affecting the scientific and medical communities, many students who originally planned on a medical career have found themselves choosing to go to law school instead. Some even go to law school after becoming a doctor.

According to surveys taken over the years, many law schools do not pay particular attention to the content of your undergraduate studies. They are more interested in your completion of college with a decent GPA, which tells them that you have the ability to focus on and achieve a long-term goal, as well as telling them how well you succeeded in achieving that goal. The LSAT, on the other hand, gives them a clear understanding of your analytical and writing skills, which will help you be successful in law school, as well as in the legal profession itself.

Preparation is the key to passing this test and achieving a good score, which is needed to secure a place in the best law schools. As with any other graduate-level specialty college, there are LSAT-specific test preparation books you may purchase and use to learn and practice with on your own. They are also available in most libraries. Over the years, these books have been a tried and true method for many law school-bound students; however, there are many LSAT preparation courses available at colleges as well.

The LSAC website (www.lsac.org) includes many good suggestions for preparing for the LSAT. This site can give you not only sample questions, but also can give you the latest trends on the test. In addition, there are many other organizations that now offer online preparation with video classes that provide a lot of good information on what to expect, as well as timed practice features. Some are even free! So, do your due diligence and Google "LSAT prep classes" to check out the variety of sites that offer LSAT preparation courses to see which would work best for you.

Remember, the LSAT is the most important factor law schools use to decide if your reasoning and analytical skills will help you succeed in law school. Therefore, this test often becomes the focus of your pre-law career. The sooner you begin preparing for this entrance exam, the better you will do on it.

Many law schools require that the LSAT be taken **by December** for admission the following fall. However, taking the test earlier is often advised, and I recommend taking the LSAT after your junior year in college, either on the June, July, or September administration dates. That way, your scores will be more likely to be available by your law school application deadline and will give you time to re-prep and retest if necessary. The LSAT is currently given six times a year, as opposed to four times a year in the past. Sign up as soon as registration dates open, as seats can fill up quickly.

The LSAC has made another change to accommodate test takers by changing the rule that limited the number of times applicants could take the LSAT. Go to www.lsac.org to keep up with these and other future LSAT changes.

The GRE as a basis for admission into law school

Some law schools are now accepting the Graduate Records Examination (GRE) as a basis for admission to law school in lieu of the LSAT. Please bear in mind that not all law schools accept the GRE alone as an entrance exam. Many do not accept it and still rely solely on the LSAT, so unless you plan on only applying to schools that do accept the GRE instead of the LSAT, I would suggest you still prepare for and take the LSAT. It is the one test that all American law schools accept. To see which law schools are accepting the GRE, check with www.ets.org.

Registering for CAS

The next step is to register for CAS (the Credential Assembly Service) which is a service provided by the LSAC. CAS will assemble a report, for a fee, which contains your transcript, LSAT scores, and letters of recommendation. After you apply to your chosen law schools, they will contact the CAS directly and request a copy of your report.

Once you have registered for CAS, you will then need to submit your transcripts and letters of recommendation to them. In choosing professors for your letters of recommendation, think about those who know you well enough to offer both positive impressions and solid predictions of your future performance as a potential law student. Using CAS is required by most ABA-approved law schools, and in the next chapter we will discuss both ABA-approved law schools as well as those non-ABA approved.

CHAPTER 2

Choosing a Law School

In this chapter...

- ✓ American Bar Association (ABA) accredited law schools
- ✓ Courses of study at ABA law schools
- ✓ Selecting a law school based upon ratings
- ✓ Accessibility of law professors

NOW THAT WE have covered the LSAT, it is time to move on to the important discussion of choosing the right law school. I was just plain lucky that I happened to pick a law school accredited by the American Bar Association (ABA). As I was already living in California, I chose to stay there and practice law. What I didn't understand was that in my home state alone there are three levels of law schools:

1. Those accredited by the American Bar Association;
2. Those accredited by the California Bar Association (CBA); and
3. Those that are non-accredited.

The above distinctions are important in that the type of law school you choose to attend may affect where you practice law upon graduation. Many states require aspiring law students to attend an ABA accredited law school. These states include Arkansas, Delaware, Idaho, Indiana, Iowa, Kansas, Mississippi, Montana, Nebraska, North Dakota, Oklahoma, South Carolina, South Dakota, and Wyoming. Other states may allow you to attend an out of state non-ABA law school, but you should definitely look into the particular state requirements before applying to a law school not accredited by the ABA. California, where I went to law school, has its own system for accrediting law schools and allows graduates of both state-accredited and non-accredited schools to take the bar alongside graduates of ABA-accredited schools.

ABA Accredited Law Schools

Graduating from a law school accredited by the ABA enables you to practice law in whichever state you choose, provided you pass the bar examination for that state. For example, if you live in Indiana and eventually want to practice law there, while at the same time want to go to law school in California, you would definitely want to go to a law school accredited by the ABA. After graduation you could then return to your home state, take the bar exam there and practice law in Indiana. If instead you chose a law school accredited by the California Bar Association, you would be limited to only taking the California Bar

Examination. You could not, even after three long, grueling years of law school return to your home state of Indiana to practice.

I did not realize the importance of this distinction in accreditation at the time I applied to law school. An attorney must be licensed to practice law in a particular state. To recap, if the school you choose to go to is ABA accredited, you can take the bar in any state you choose; however, if you go to, say, a California bar accredited school (or one accredited in one of the other few states that follow California's model), you are restricted to practicing only in that state for a number of years afterward before you are eligible to take the new state's bar exam.

If you are unsure if a law school you are interested in is accredited by the ABA, you can call the ABA to get the information you need. The ABA also maintains a detailed, current list of over 200 ABA accredited law schools at https://bit.ly/2x-QBKZ3. This alphabetical list is comprised of links that connect you to each school's individual website and includes the year of their accreditation. Each school's website lists admission requirements, financial assistance, faculty, and details on the facilities. If you click on the link for **"ABA Required Disclosures"** you can find information on scholarship retention data, transfer of credit policies, refund policies, curriculum, academic calendar, and academic requirements. All ABA accredited schools must provide this information on their website, and it can usually be found in the footer area of the page along with other links to web pages helpful to incoming or current students, as well as to alumni. In addition, the LSAC also offers a free "Official Guide to ABA-approved Law Schools" which you can find at www. officialguide.lsac.org.

I am passing this information on to you because I was not aware of it when I was applying to law schools. Knowing the difference between attending a law school accredited by the ABA and one accredited by the California Bar Association (or any other state bar association) could have tremendous consequences on your future law career.

Course of Study at ABA Law Schools

Since I went to a law school accredited by the ABA, we studied, among other things, the **common law**, which is the statutory and case law background of England and the American colonies prior to the American Revolution, as well as the case law of the United States since the American Revolution. When I entered my first year of law school I had no idea what the common law was. Nor did I really understand the difference between case law and statutory law. **Case law**, the bulk of your first year reading, is the rules of law found in court decisions. **Statutory law,** on the other hand, consists of laws enacted by state legislatures and, at the federal level, by Congress.

A simple example of a law created by state statute is the requirement by all states that members of certain professions must obtain licenses allowing them to practice their chosen profession. Lawyers are but a few of the people who must be licensed. There are fifty states in the United States, and each of them has a different history and, therefore, different laws.

One of the reasons you are limited to practice in California upon graduating from a school accredited by the California Bar Examination is that those schools mainly focus on the case and statutory law of California, rather than the laws of the various fifty states. Hopefully, you can see why going to a law school accredited by the ABA rather than a school only accredited by a state bar association should be an important part of your decision as to which schools you wish to apply.

Now, let me briefly warn you about attending a non-accredited law school. Virtually *anybody* can start a law school and teach law; therefore, you must seriously investigate any school that is non-accredited to make sure that its courses meet the requirements for taking the bar examination of your future choice.

Selecting a Law School Based Upon Ratings

There are many institutions which offer law programs, and if a particular field of law interests you, then you should target schools that are particularly strong in that area. All law schools teach the same skills and courses in the first year, but after that you can choose from a variety of electives in your area of interest. In addition, the ratings given by *US News & World Report* are a good resource when selecting a law school. *The Princeton Review* is another resource that ranks law schools based on data from surveys of tens of thousands of students attending the schools and of school administrators as well. The quality of the pool of applicants depends on the rating of the law school. Thus, many students self-select a law school based on their grades and LSAT scores as well as choosing the highest-ranking law school that makes sense from a financial perspective.

Accessibility of Law Professors

One last thing to consider when choosing a law school is the accessibility of your professors. Law professors typically engage in three kinds of activities: research, teaching, and public service. The main research work in law involves the publication of articles in law reviews, although many professors write books and edit casebooks as well. Law schools also require faculty to teach.

Many professors have open door policies with students, while others maintain minimum contact with students outside of class. At Pepperdine, there was, and still is, a true connection between professors and students, with a horizontal versus a vertical relationship. Many other law schools have such a strong connection between students and their professors, while others do not. A good resource to determine the accessibility of professors outside the classroom is *The Princeton Review*.

Now that we have discussed the preliminaries of the law school admissions process and choosing the right law school, let's delve into the first year law experience.

PART II

B is for Behind-the-Scenes of Your First Year

CHAPTER 3

The First Day

In this chapter...

✓ Sample first year schedule
✓ Fundamental first year classes
✓ Current trends in law school instruction

I ARRIVED ON campus the first day and was greeted by a note telling me that I had been assigned to Section A. I had been assigned a faculty advisor, and my schedule of classes was enclosed. It looked like this: (See Table 3.1 on the following page.)

Ref. No.	Course Number & Title (Units)	Time	Day	Room	Time	& Date
FIRST YEAR SECTION A **FALL / 1984**						
20933 753	Civil Pleadings & Procedure I (3 units)	1:15–2:15	MTTH	C	9:00 M	12/10
20776 603	Contracts I (3 units)	10:45–11:45	MWF	C	9:00 M	12/17
20800 622	Criminal Law (2 units)	9:30–10:30	TTH	C	9:00 F	12/14
20867 703	Real Property I (3 units)	2:30–3:30	T	C	9:00 W	12/19
		1:15–2:15	WF			
20834 653	Torts I (3 units)	8:15–9:15	MWF	C	9:00 W	12/12
20669 181	Legal Research & Writing (1 ½ units)	9:30–10:30	MW	S3&4		
SPRING / 1985						
762	Civil Pleading & Procedure (2)	1:15–2:15	TTH	C	9:00 T	4/30
613	Contracts II (3)	10:45–11:45	MWF	C	9:00 M	5/6
822	Criminal Procedure (3)	1:15–2:15	M	C	9:00 W	5/8
713	Real Property II (3)	9:30–10:30	TTH	C	9:00 F	5/10
633	Torts II (3)	8:15–9:15	MWF	C	9:00 Th	5/2
181	Legal Research & Writing (1 ½ units)	TBA				

Table 3.1

When I first reviewed the ominous looking schedule in Table 3.1, I noticed two constraints. First, all my core classes were to be in room C (wherever that was) and, second, all of my final exams were to start at 9:00 a.m. Other than that, all I could think was, "how in the world can I handle it?" Suffice it to say, I did handle it, and so can you. My aim with this book is to make it a little easier for you to succeed by sharing my own experience, strength, and hope.

Some schools include Constitutional Law as a first year core class, while others reserve it for upper division students. It was not included in the first year schedule of classes when I was in law school, so I didn't take Constitutional Law until my second year. However, I include a discussion of that class in my diary since this all-important subject is covered on the bar examination and is currently covered in the first year curriculum of most law schools.

To show you how much things change while also staying the same, Table 3.2 details a **current** schedule of classes at my alma mater as of this writing. Pepperdine now includes a semester of Constitutional Law (called Constitutional Structure) during the first year, and also has added a course called Introduction to Ethical Lawyering, in addition to the core classes of Civil Procedure, Contracts, Criminal Law, Legal Research and Writing, Real Property, and Torts.

Here is a sample schedule of a first year law student at Pepperdine during the 2017/18 academic year.

FIRST YEAR SECTION A / SPRING / 2017		
Course Number & Title (Units)	Time	Day
Civil Procedure (5 units)	1:40–3:20	MTTH
Torts (5 units)	9:10-10:50	MWF
Legal Research & Writing (2 units)	10:20-11:20	TTH
Constitutional Structure (2 units)	11:30-12:30	TTH
Experiential Exam Workshop	TBD	TH
Intro to Professional Formation Training	TBD	T
FIRST YEAR SECTION A / FALL / 2018		
Contracts (5 units)	10:50–12:30	MWF
Criminal Law (3 units)	1:40–3:10	MW
Real Property (5 units)	3:20-4:50	M
	1:40-3:20	TTH
Legal Research & Writing (2 units)	10:20-11:20	TTH
Intro to Professional Formation	TBD	TBD

Table 3.2

Fundamental First Year Classes

Most law schools teach the same core subjects and then give the students the opportunity to study various electives of their choice during their second and third year of law school. These fundamental first year classes typically include:

1. Torts;
2. Legal Research and Writing;
3. Contracts;
4. Civil Procedure;
5. Criminal Law;
6. Real Property; and
7. Constitutional Law.

These subjects not only form the basis of instruction for first year law students, but are also tested on the bar examination. In other words, the first year curriculum is the cornerstone of your law school education, and no matter which law school you end up at, you can expect to study all of the above courses.

After the first year, current students at Pepperdine are required to complete 18-21 units of additional courses, including: Corporations, Criminal Procedure, Evidence, Federal Income Taxation, Remedies, and Wills and Trusts. When I was in law school, I took one semester of Criminal Law and one of Criminal Procedure during my first year; this has since changed, and Criminal Procedure is now offered as an upper division course. As you can see from Table 3.2, the same basic classes are still taught as when I was in school, but the number of units and length of the courses has changed.

Current trends in law school instruction

The current trend is towards consolidation. In my first year, we covered Civil Procedure, Contracts, Real Property, Torts, and Legal Research and Writing in two semesters. Currently, all these classes, with the exception of Legal Research & Writing, are taught in one semester. Thus, the units given for the classes are different, as well as the time spent in class. In addition, the Intro to Professional Formation class has been added and includes sessions in the spring term to prepare students for summer jobs. I also want to point out that letter grades are now given at Pepperdine, as opposed to number grades given when I was there.

Consolidating a course that was traditionally a two-semester course into one semester does not mean the amount of information you must learn and be responsible for has lessened. Unfortunately, the number of legal concepts you need to learn is continually increasing as the body of law in our society expands. To add to this, the time constraints faced by professors in which to teach a given subject places more responsibility on the students' shoulders when reading and assimilating information that may only be glossed over in class. In other words, you must be thorough and organized in your study habits to successfully absorb the material necessary to pass the course and, eventually, the bar exam.

On the positive side, recent changes to Pepperdine's instructional programs actually include a couple of unique schedule offerings, such as an increased number of night classes and summer session classes. Working students also now have the option of extending the length of their Juris Doctorate (JD) program to four years so that they can better balance a lower workload of classes with their jobs. Additionally, for those students who wish to take on a heavier class schedule, it is now possible to complete their JD in two years!

As you can see, with law schools such as Pepperdine considering the practical needs of the students seeking a law degree, the instructional model is becoming much more flexible. Despite this, the same core classes are covered during the first year, so you need to be prepared.

And now on to my first class: Torts.

CHAPTER 4

Torts

In this chapter...

- ✓ What is a tort?
- ✓ Socratic method of teaching law
- ✓ IRAC method
- ✓ Overview of tort law
- ✓ Intentional torts
- ✓ Negligence
- ✓ Strict liability torts

TORTS WAS THE first class on my schedule. I arrived early for my 8:15 a.m. class so that I could actually figure out where classroom C was. I was a nervous wreck, as were my fellow classmates. However, I was so self-absorbed in my own fearful expectations that I didn't realize they were as scared as I was.

What is a Tort?

To begin with, I had no idea what a tort actually was. The title of the class sounded more like a French pastry to me than a law school class. Actually, I was not far off in that the word "tort" as we use it in English is derived from a French word, although instead of describing a type of pastry, it means "an injury or wrong." The French word originally comes from the Latin word *tortus*, which means "twisted."

In terms of the law, a **tort** is basically a wrong. Specifically, it is a private or civil wrong or injury which results from a breach of legal duty that exists due to society's expectations regarding our conduct with others. A tort is different from a contract or other private relationship, as we will see later on when I discuss my contracts class. On that first day of class, however, I had no idea what this really meant.

At first, I was surprised that we didn't get much explanation from the professor as to what constituted the body of law called torts. I quickly learned that the professor expected us to figure it out by reading the case law in our textbook, which was unlike any other textbook I had ever encountered. Most textbooks give information in a straight-forward manner. Not so with law books. Instead of simply explaining the legal doctrine involved (in this instance, giving a straightforward definition of a tort), our textbook contained excerpts from legal cases in which the law of that particular area of study was applied. This casebook method of teaching the law is designed to teach law students how to think like a lawyer and how to extrapolate important concepts and ideas from studying actual court decisions. At first, however, the process can be very daunting.

Our textbook was entitled *Cases and Materials on Torts*, by Wade, Schwartz, Kelly and Paulette. This title is still one of the standard books used to teach the law of torts to first year students. Reading the first case illustrates the previous point about how legal textbooks in law school are different than those you encounter in college. It was an unnamed case dated 1466, which has subsequently been dubbed, "The Case of the Thorns." This is one of the earliest known English torts cases and, while no documentation of the original case exists today, it has been preserved in various forms in a number of texts through the centuries. The version I have included here is from the summary of the case as set out in *Bessey v. Olliot & Lambert*, T. Raym. 467 (1681).

The Case Of The Thorns, Y.B. 6 Ed. 4, f. 7, pl. 18 (K.B. 1466)

A man brought a writ of Trespass *quare vi et armis clausum fregit, & herban suam pedibus conculcando consumpsit* in five Acres. The Defendant pleads, that he hath an Acre lying next the said five Acres, and upon it a hedge of Thorns, and he cut the Thorns, and they, against his will, fell upon the Plaintiff's Land, and the Defendant took them off as soon as he could, which is the same Trespass; and the Plaintiff demurred; and adjudged for the Plaintiff; for though a Man doth a lawful Thing, yet if any damage do thereby befall another, he shall answer for it, if he could have avoided it. As if a Man lop a Tree, and the boughs fall upon another against his will yet an Action lies. If a Man shoot at the Butts, and hurt another unawares, an Action lies. I have Land through which a River runs to your Mill, and I lop the the Sallows growing upon the Riverside, which accidentally stop the Water, so as your Mill is hindered, an Action lies. If I am Building my own house, and a Piece of Timber falls on my Neighbour's house and breaks Part of it, an Action lies. If a Man assault me, and I lift up my Staff to defend myself, and in lifting it up hit another, an Action lies by that Person, and yet I did a lawful Thing. And the Reason of all these Cases is because he that is damage ought to be recompensed. But otherwise it is in Criminal Cases, for there *actus non facit reum nisi mens sit rea.*

(The Latin phrase *herban suam pedibus conculcando consumpsit*, roughly translated, means "trampled and damaged the vegetation." And the Latin phrase

actus non facit reum nisi mens sit rea, **roughly translated, means "an act does not make one guilty unless there be a guilty mind.")**

After re-reading this case several times, I gathered that the defendant was sued for trespassing on the plaintiff's land when he went to recover the branches of a hedge of thorns that had fallen while he was cutting the hedge; however, I was no closer to having a clear picture of what a tort was. Since my professor seemingly spent more time asking questions than teaching, I spent countless hours that first semester sifting through voluminous cases, seeking out important concepts that kept eluding me.

I had run up against the first hurdle of law school. I was used to having things spelled out for me in class by my professors. In the typical undergraduate classroom experience, students sit through an hour or two of lectures during which the professor lists and describes the subject matter that will be on the final exam. Students typically take notes on what the professor says, study the relevant points, and often memorize large portions of their textbooks in preparation for exams. Not so in the realm of law school.

Socratic Method of Teaching Law

Most classes in law school are taught using the **Socratic method** of instruction. Law school students are expected to have already read and assimilated the assigned text and be prepared to discuss it in class. During the typical law school class, the professor asks analytical questions on the cases you have read for homework. This particular method of instruction is very nerve-wracking at first. But as time goes on, the reason for this style of teaching is obvious. Not only does it help keep students on their toes when it comes to preparing for (and staying awake during) class, but it also teaches them to think critically about the law.

The professor becomes an exemplar, using his questions to teach students to use their own reasoning skills and observation to analyze a case's set of facts and apply existing law to those facts. Interestingly, there may be no right or wrong answer to any of the questions the professor asks. The process of teaching in this manner sets up a dynamic method of analysis that will assist future attorneys in applying arguments to the law throughout their careers.

On the first day of class, I was terrified when the professor called my name and then asked me to tell him the facts of *Weaver v. Ward*, 80 Eng. Rep. 284 (K.B. 1616). I had read the case, but it was written in 1616 and for the life of me I couldn't figure out why it was in the textbook at all. But I swallowed hard and then told him as concisely as I could that the facts of the case were that Ward's gun injured Weaver when it accidentally discharged during military maneuvers.

IRAC Method

I'd like to go over the **IRAC** method at this point and explain how it applies to the *Weaver v. Ward* case. You will be introduced during your first year of law school to this universal method of organizing your answers in law school essay questions and to analyze cases as well. This framework is not only the mainstay of final exams, but also of the bar examination and legal writing in general.

The letter **"I"** stands for the **Issue** of the case. In *Weaver v. Ward*, the issue was whether one is excused for an injury caused without fault. The issue of a case always starts with a question and a good way to start the question is with the word "whether." You can often find the issue stated directly in the cases you are reading.

The initial **"R"** stands for the **Rule of Law** in the case. The rule of law in the *Weaver* case was that one can be excused from liability for injuries caused by no fault of the wrongdoer.

Before getting to the third letter of the acronym for IRAC, I have to admit I was overwhelmed by the language of tort law, and it was only my first week of school. Being liable or being excused from tort liability? What in the world did that really mean? Let me try to explain it to you in simpler terms.

Liability means responsibility for one's conduct. Thus, a person is either responsible for his actions and held accountable in tort law or he is excused from responsibility. A **tortfeasor** is one who commits a tort, while **tortious** describes conduct which subjects a person to tort liability.

Let's get back to our discussion of the **IRAC** approach; the next initial **"A"** stands for the **Analysis** of the case. Continuing with our discussion of *Weaver v. Ward*, the analysis would entail a discussion of the facts of the case using the applicable rule of law. An injury definitely occurred as Weaver was hurt when

Ward's gun accidentally fired. The only question is *whether* or not Ward can be held legally responsible for his accidental conduct.

The initial **"C"** stands for the **Conclusion** of the case. Since the rule of law is that one may be excused from one's accidental conduct, the conclusion would be that Ward was not liable for the injuries sustained by Weaver when his gun accidentally discharged. In other words, we are held responsible for our conduct in society; however, there are cases where the law may excuse that responsibility, as in the above instance. It's helpful to use a template similar to that in Table 4.1 for using the IRAC method of analysis.

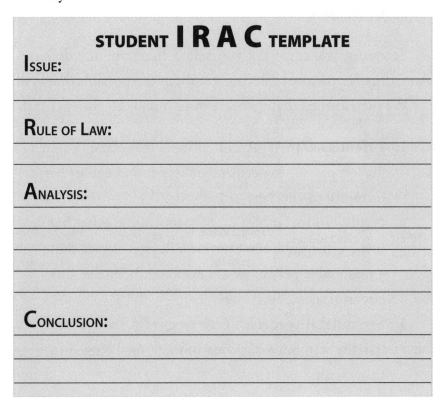

STUDENT I R A C TEMPLATE

ISSUE:

RULE OF LAW:

ANALYSIS:

CONCLUSION:

Table 4.1

Overview of Tort Law

We spent the next several weeks in our Torts class dealing with the development of liability based upon fault. We studied the above concept through discussing the cases in our textbook. The main ideas I distilled from these discussions were as follows.

Firstly, when dealing with a tort you must first decide whether the elements of a tort are present. Those elements are:

1. **Act**;
2. **Intent**; and
3. **Causation**.

Secondly, you must ask yourself if there are any defenses. And, thirdly, you must ask yourself about the possible damages.

We then learned that there are three broad categories of torts:

1. **Intentional torts:** An intentional tort occurs when a person *intends* to perform an action that causes harm or injury to another;
2. **Negligent torts:** Negligent torts, on the other hand, involve the failure to exercise a degree of care that a reasonable person would exercise under the same circumstances; and
3. **Strict liability torts:** These types of torts refer to liability without a showing of fault, or the need to show fault.

The rest of the year in my Torts class focused on the specifics of these preliminary concepts. If you can grasp them, you are well on your way to understanding the vast realm of tort law. In other words, the cases I read those first weeks of school all had to do with these rudiments of tort law.

We had three essay questions on our Torts first semester final examination, and they all dealt with some aspect of negligence, intentional torts, and strict liability. Question III had a fact pattern that dealt with negligent repair, trespassing, breach of duty, negligent failure to act, and false imprisonment. As you can see in Table 4.2 on the following page, I missed a lot of issues, and my raw score on this third question was 65, with an actual score of 77. Most of my professors did not give us the exam questions to keep, but my professor did give us an exam key so that we could visually see how we did on the essay in comparison to what he was looking for us to discuss.

Needless to say, I was frustrated and disappointed at this point, but I grew more accustomed to how to spot issues and improve my exam writing as the year progressed. Afterwards, I learned a very helpful mnemonic learning device for tackling torts questions that I discuss in the Torts outline later in this book.

By the time I graduated, I was in the top 25% of my class. I share this with you so that you don't get too overwhelmed or anxious if you don't get top grades your first semester of law school.

EXAM KEY - QUESTION III

✓ PETE V. DAN - NEGLIGENT REPAIR
✓ What was Dan's duty of repair, if any, to Pete?
___ Was Pete a trespasser?
___ Trespasser need not know land belongs to another
___ If Pete acted under private necessity, no trespass
___ Here, necessity is questionable
✓ Generally no duty to unknown trespasser
✓ Developing duty of reasonable care to all (Rowland)
✓ Some do not extend Rowland to trespassers
✓ Did Pete breach a duty by violating the statute?
___ Administrative regulation may est. neg. per se
✓ Ad. Reg. to prevent this harm, to this class of persons
✓ Possibly not designed to protect trespasser
___ Ad. Reg. may be only evidence of negligence
___ Ad. Reg. often given less weight than statute (p. 235, n. 6)
___ Ad. Reg. should have less weight - not elected
___ Ad. Reg. should have greater weight - more expert
✓ Did Dan breach a duty by acting unreasonably?
___ Reasonableness - Burden of repair
2 Reasonableness - Probability x Loss
___ Was Dan's repair the proximate cause of Pete's initial injury?
3 Must be one foreseeably injured - Cardozo
___ Was Dan's repair the proximate cause of Pete's increased injury?
___ Increased injury - second accident

✓ PETE V. DAN - NEGLIGENT FAILURE TO ACT
✓ Duty to act, def.'s instrumentality causes injury w/o neg. (p. 142)
✓ Liable for increased injury for failure to act

___ PETE V. DAN - FALSE IMPRISONMENT, FAILURE TO ACT
___ Confined - Unreasonable means of escape (p. 39)
___ Intentional failure to act in face of duty to act (p. 47)

✓ Well Written

65 Raw Score

77 Actual Score, this question

Table 4.2

Intentional Torts

Next, let's briefly go over some common examples of the three categories of torts, so that you have a better understanding of what to expect in a Torts class. Two **intentional** torts we studied included **assault** and **battery**. There are many others which are listed in the Torts outline later on in the Appendix/Outlines section of this book.

An **assault** is defined as any intentional, unexcused act that creates in another person a reasonable *apprehension* of immediate harmful contact. This is in contrast to **battery**, which is any unexcused harmful or offensive *physical contact* intentionally performed. For an assault to occur there only needs to be apprehension by the victim of physical contact, while for a battery to occur there must be actual physical contact.

Torts are classified under **civil law,** rather than **criminal law.** This means that some torts may involve conduct that is not necessarily illegal, but causes harm to another person; however, some tort cases may overlap with criminal law, such as assault and battery. Another tort that overlaps with criminal law is **trespass,** which is defined as knowingly entering another person's property without permission. We also studied trespass in depth in my real property first year class. Under tort law, a property owner may bring a civil lawsuit against a trespasser in order to recover damages or receive compensatory relief for an injury suffered as a direct result of trespass. Under criminal law, criminal charges ranging from a minor violation to a felony may be brought against someone who interferes with another person's legal property rights.

NEGLIGENCE

Torts can also be unintentional, such as **negligence**; this is the most common type of tort lawsuit, such as a slip and fall case. For example, if a store owner had a duty to keep their store floor clean but failed to do so, a customer may be able to sue them if he or she was injured due to slipping on the dirty store floor. In order to prove negligence, the victim needs to prove that the defendant breached a **duty of care** owed to them, and that the breach was the cause of their injuries or losses.

STRICT LIABILITY TORTS

Strict liability is the imposition of liability without a finding of fault. Contrast this to intentional and negligent torts, where there must be fault on the part of the wrongdoer for liability to be imposed. For strict liability to occur, the plaintiff only needs to prove that the tort occurred and that the defendant was responsible. The law attributes strict liability to situations deemed to be inherently dangerous. When people participate in **ultrahazardous activities**, they may be held liable when another person is injured. Examples of such actions include keeping wild animals, using explosives, and making defective products.

Here is a visual to help you understand the theories of liability we have discussed.

TORT LAW LIABILITY	
FAULT	**NO FAULT**
Intentional Torts	Strict Liability
Negligence	

TABLE 4.3

The above brief examples of the types of torts we studied during the first year of law school are not meant to be an exhaustive list. Rather, I just want to familiarize you with the over-all picture so that you will have more clarity and understanding of this important area of civil law. Let's continue on our journey of learning the *ABCs of Law School* with the next class on my schedule which was Legal Research and Writing.

CHAPTER 5

Legal Research and Writing

In this chapter...

✓ Substantive v. procedural law
✓ 3 basic sources of law
✓ How to find statutory law
✓ State statutes
✓ Federal statutes
✓ How to find state court decisions
✓ How to find federal court decisions
✓ Binding v. persuasive authority
✓ How to find administrative law
✓ Shepardizing
✓ Citations

LET'S SHIFT GEARS, which is something I had to do very often during my first year of law school. Just as I was beginning to get the hang of what the law of torts was all about, I had to think about Legal Research and Writing. That class was the next one on my schedule for Monday morning. I had a fifteen-minute break to grab a cup of coffee and find my way to rooms S3 and S4.

Since the Legal Research and Writing program was broken down into groups, we had a smaller classroom and fewer students. In this setting, I began to look around the room at a sampling of my fellow colleagues. Some looked as though they would someday be litigators, while others appeared to be the perfect fit for a Big Law junior associate position upon graduation. Then there were those whom I felt were in law school with the altruistic vision of changing the world. And as the instructor entered the room, I wondered what *this* teacher would expect of us.

He quickly introduced himself and began talking about the subject of Legal Research and Writing. I learned that, although this class was most probably my only break from the Socratic method, it was going to require a lot of prep time outside of the classroom.

He explained how this course was different than the other core first year classes. Instead of studying substantive law and procedural law, we were going to learn how to find the law in the law library and write legal papers based upon it. In other words, this course is designed to help law students acquire fundamental skills in legal research, analysis, and writing. On an aside, many law schools call this course other names such as "Legal Method" or "Writing or Elements of the Law."

That made sense to me except for one thing: what in the world did he mean by substantive and procedural law? Let me explain it to you.

Substantive v. Procedural Law

Substantive law is the body of laws that structure and govern the members of our society. It defines rights and responsibilities in civil law and crimes and punishments in criminal law. It may be codified in statutes or exist through precedents in common law. Examples of substantive law include torts, contracts, wills, penal codes, and real property.

Procedural law is the set of procedures used for making, administering, and enforcing substantive law. It is the rules that define how courts hear and resolve lawsuits (civil), as well as those that govern criminal and administrative proceedings. These procedures are designed to ensure a fair and impartial hearing of any matter that comes before a court so as to enforce the rights to due process of both the individual and the state.

Both substantive and procedural law are affected by Supreme Court opinions and are subject to constitutional interpretations; however, each serves a different function in our justice system.

3 Basic Sources of the Law

At this point, we went on our first of many tours of the law library. As I mentioned earlier, legal research and writing was definitely not my strong suit during my first months of law school. However, with practice and more understanding my writing definitely improved.

We learned that there are three basic sources of law:

1. **Codes;**
2. **Case law;** and
3. **Administrative law** (the decisions of administrative agencies)

On our first library tour we focused on finding out where the various codes were kept. The main sources of law are the United States Constitution and the individual state constitutions. Those documents can supersede state codes, case law, and administrative law. More on that when we talk about my experience with Constitutional Law.

Codes, also known as statutes, are enacted by Congress and the various state legislative bodies. They are collectively referred to as **statutory law.** Statutory law is central to many legal issues and should often be the starting point for much of your research.

State Statutes

Since my law school was in California, we went directly to the section of our law library dealing with California codes. There are forty-seven codes in California dealing with just about every aspect of life. The legislature rules on these various aspects are found in the codes. Some examples of codes in California include the *California Vehicle Code*, the *Penal Code*, the *Business Code*, the *Evidence Code*, and the *Code of Civil Procedure*. Each state has an official version of its own codes. In addition, commercial publishers may produce unofficial versions of state codes. Both the official and unofficial codes will include the full text of all the state's statutory law, but many times the unofficial codes will include annotations which provide reference to case law and other materials that cite a particular code section. We learned how to use these codes in our research projects.

Federal Statutes

After the United States Congress passes a bill and the President signs it into law, it is typically **codified.** This means that it is placed into the United States Code (USC), the official version of federal statutory law. The **USC** includes 50 subject titles, which are subdivided into chapters and sections. Since 1927, West has published an annotated version of the USC, the United States Code Annotated® (USCA®).

Case Law

Since I had just spent an hour before this library tour dealing with cases from my Torts textbook, I was much more interested in learning about the second source of law, namely **case law**. Case law is derived from actual lawsuits, rather than from statutes or codes.

Most state trial court decisions are not published, although the municipal and superior court records of individual cases are available to the public upon request once a trial is concluded. In most states, trials usually begin on the county level and many county courts maintain searchable websites for information pertaining to active or decided public cases. In addition, most trials are open to the public at the time the case is being tried in court, unless publicity of the trial prevents the parties involved from receiving a fair trial.

How to Find State Court Decisions

The written decisions of state appellate courts are published and contained in **reports**. An **appellate court,** also known as an **appeals court**, is a court having the authority to review the law applied by a lower court in the same case. In most cases, the trial court first decides a lawsuit or reaches a verdict in a criminal trial. A **review** of its decision can then be requested through an appellate court.

Appellate rules and the processes of vary greatly from state to state. Depending on the state rules and the circumstances of the trial, appeals can be based on questions of the errors of the law, facts, procedure, or due process. In general, one cannot appeal simply because one does not agree with the decision.

An **appellant** is the party to a lawsuit who appeals a lower court decision to a higher court. Often the appellant is referred to as the **petitioner**. An **appellee**, on the other hand, is the party prevailing in the lower court who argues, on appeal, against setting aside the ruling of the lower court. In some state courts this party is called the **respondent**.

The above terms are important to understand your first year of law school because they crop up in many of the cases in your various course textbooks. The professor will often ask you who the appellant or appellee is in a particular case.

The court's decisions are usually published at the direction of the court and contain the **opinion** (the court's reason for its decision), the rules of law that apply to the case, and the judgment. The **judgment** is the court's determination of the rights of the parties. The court's decision or judgment either reinforces, changes, establishes, or overturns legal precedent.

The published opinions of appellate courts constitute one of the major sources of law in our legal system. If all the appellate justices or judges reviewing a case do not agree, a **majority opinion** is written which gives the viewpoint of the majority of justices or judges. The majority opinion is the official law. Often a **concurring opinion** is written if one of the judges or justices feels strongly about emphasizing a particular point. Lastly, a **dissenting opinion** is written by a judge or justice who disagrees with the majority opinion. Thus, case law is known as judge-made law in that it has developed from judgments handed down in court. Judges decide cases along the lines of earlier decisions made in similar cases.

The decisions of state courts are collected in **state case reporters**. Many state court opinions are also published by West Publishing Company and are available online through Westlaw and Lexis in a series of reporters called **regional reporters**. These reprint the full text of opinions from courts in a specific geographical area of the country. For example, California cases, along with cases from Alaska, Arizona, Colorado, Hawaii, Idaho, Kansas, Montana, Nevada, New Mexico, Oklahoma, Oregon, Utah, Washington, and Wyoming, are found in the *Pacific Reporter*.

The law on a particular subject can also be found through **case digests**. Digests contain a collection of the law according to topics and subject matter. They function as an index to the court reports, which are almost always published in chronological order, and provide brief summaries of the opinions reported.

How to Find Federal Court Decisions

We found out that each federal court also has a case reporter for its decisions. Those cases decided by the United States Supreme Court are contained in a series of books called the *United States Reports* (abbreviated U.S.).

In addition, there are two unofficial reporters that also contain the decisions of the United States Supreme Court. These are:

1. *The Supreme Court Reporter* (S.Ct.), published by West Publishing Company; and
2. *The United States Supreme Court Reports, Lawyer's Edition* (L.Ed. And L.Ed.2d) published by Lawyers Cooperative Publishing Company.

These unofficial reporters contain the same information as the official reports; the difference is that the unofficial reporters also contain commentaries and editorial remarks.

The United States Courts of Appeal decisions from all circuits are found in the *Federal Reporter*. These reporters contain decisions of the federal intermediate appellate courts. There are thirteen federal courts of appeal, each of which covers a geographical area called a **circuit**. For easy reference, I discovered that there is a list at the beginning of each volume of the federal reporters showing all the courts whose decisions are reported in that volume. For example, California is in the Ninth Circuit of the U. S. Court of Appeals. Thus, one can find the common law in case reporters, both at the federal and state levels.

The United States District Courts are the trial courts in our federal system. They decide the facts of a given dispute and what those facts mean in relation to the relevant law. Thus, the District Courts, Courts of Appeals, and the Supreme Court are the courts whose opinions lawyers and judges rely on at the federal level. However, in everyday practice, attorneys are predominantly reliant on state law.

Binding v. Persuasive Authority

We also learned about the difference between binding and persuasive authority. **Binding authority** means that the lower courts must follow the rulings of higher courts in their jurisdiction. Contrast **persuasive authority**, where the court considers the reasoning of another court or other sources of law in deciding, but the judge is not bound by precedent when making a decision. In other words, courts are required to follow the decisions of higher courts in the same jurisdiction but are not required to follow decisions from courts in other jurisdictions. Both federal and state courts are bound by the decisions of the U.S. Supreme Court on U.S. constitutional and other issues of federal law.

Typically, state courts are bound by the decisions of the higher courts in that specific state. For example, in California, the trial courts are bound by the opinions issued by the California Courts of Appeals and the California Supreme Court; however, courts in California are not bound by the decisions of other state courts, such as Nevada.

How to Find Administrative Law

Now, let's discuss the third source of law, the decisions of administrative agencies. Normally, there are three separate sources of governmental power in the United States, each with its own checks and balances. These are:

1. The **legislative branch,** which makes the laws;
2. The **judicial branch**, which interprets the laws; and
3. The **executive branch,** which enforces the laws.

Administrative agencies are created when the various branches of the government delegate some of their authority to a group of persons designated as experts in that particular field. These experts constitute an administrative agency. These agencies have a tremendous amount of power within the scope of their designated purpose and authority as there is no true separation of power. However, in 1946, Congress enacted the **Administrative Procedure Act (APA),** which is the federal statute that governs the way administrative agencies may create regulations.

Because this statute was created to protect the rights of citizens to due process, many of these agencies follow the same organization as the federal government in that they "legislate" through rulemaking, "execute" administrative goals through agency enforcement personnel, and "adjudicate" through administrative hearings. Besides the APA, agencies draw on three other sources of authority to create internal procedures: organic statutes that define its authority and responsibility, agency rules, and informal agency practice.

Examples of administrative agencies within federal and state systems include the Securities and Exchange Commission (SEC) and the Department of Motor Vehicles (DMV).

Administrative rules are often arranged chronologically in **administrative registers**, such as the *Federal Register*, and according to subject matter in administrative codes, such as the *Code of Federal Regulations*. Administrative agencies also produce guidance documents to assist with rule writing.

I know that all of this is a lot of information to digest, but it is important to understand the structure of government and how it relates to legal research sources. This understanding helped make my research more methodical and efficient.

Shepardizing

Our Legal Research and Writing instructor also emphasized the importance of **Shepardizing** before citing a statute or a case as authority. I had no idea what that meant, but it is actually a simple concept which means you must verify that what you are citing is still 'good law' and has not been overruled, modified or excessively criticized. The process is named for Frank Shepard, a nineteenth century legal publisher who developed a method of indexing all of the citations that referred to a given case. Initially, Shepard's indexes were produced in book form and these books can still be found in law libraries and in major public libraries throughout the United States. We found the sets of Shepard's on our library tour, but they can also be found electronically through Lexis and Westlaw. Today, most attorneys use the online versions for their convenience. There are a number of other online services that provide Shepardizing tools, but, in general, they do not provide the comprehensive Shepardizing functions offered by Westlaw and LexisNexis.

Are you feeling overwhelmed yet? You're in good company. I spent an entire semester studying the above concepts in depth. However, my Legal Research and Writing class definitely made more sense as I began to see how it related to my law books and cases therein.

Citations

Before leaving the topic of legal research, a brief mention of citations is merited. **Citations** are a form of shorthand notation used to identify and locate a particular source of law. They are used for both **briefs**, which are legal documents presented to a court arguing why one party to a case should prevail, and **legal memorandums**, which are informal documents used to aid the parties involved in a legal matter in remembering particular points of law and facts. They are also used in **law review footnotes**. A law review is a student-run journal that publishes articles written by law professors, judges, and other legal professionals. Many law reviews also publish shorter pieces written by law students called "notes" or "comments."

The Bluebook: A Uniform System of Citation, commonly referred to as *The Bluebook*, is the legal community's bible for correct basic citation forms. Becoming familiar with this book will aid you in law school and in your future employment as an attorney. In addition, many states publish their own style manuals and recommend the standards of *The Bluebook* be used for federal cases, while the state's style manual standards be used for state cases. Often the state style manual clarifies certain types of citations or parts of citations that *The Bluebook* does not mention. The purpose of these books is to provide a standard format with which the various levels of the legal community can quickly and accurately reference case law in their communications.

A citation identifies the legal authority or reference such as the Constitution, statute, court decision or administrative rule. For example, a typical case citation includes the name of the case, the published sources in which you can find the case, the year the decision was rendered, and the prior or subsequent history of the case.

Let's look at the following case citation and then analyze it together.

Kubrick v. United States, 581 F.2d 1092 (3d Cir. 1978), aff'g 435 F. Supp. 166 (E.D. Pa. 1977), rev'd 444 U.S. 11 (1979).

The title of the above case is "Kubrick v. United States." Kubrick is the appellant or petitioner and the United States is the appellee or respondent. The "v." stands for *versus*, a Latin word that means "against." The title of the case designates the names of the parties to the lawsuit and is often referred to as the **style** of the case. When a case is appealed, the appellate court places the name of the party appealing the decision first. According to *The Bluebook*, the case name may be underlined or italicized, depending on use, however, the trend in recent years is to italicize the case name.

In the above citation, "581 F.2d 1092 (3d Cir. 1978)" is the published source where you can find this case. The number "581" is the volume number of "F.2d," the second series of the *Federal Reporter*, and "1092" refers to the page number in that particular volume.

As we learned earlier, the *Federal Reporter* (abbreviated "F." for the first series and "F.2d" for the second series) contains cases from the United States Court of Appeals and that cases after 1924 are published in the F.2d series. The "3d Cir." notation in parentheses refers to the third circuit of the United States Court of Appeals.

The rest of the citation refers to both the prior and the subsequent history of the case. The prior history is given first as seen in "aff'g 435 F. Supp. 166 (E.D. Pa 1977)." The abbreviation "aff'g" means that the court reviewing the case was "affirming" the original decision of the lower court and the rest of that portion of the citation refers to that case. Again, "435" refers to the volume of the Federal Supplement ("F.Supp."), which contains the opinions of the United States District Court since 1938, and "166" refers to the page number in that particular volume. The information contained in parentheses "(E.D. Pa. 1977)" refers to the Eastern District of Pennsylvania and the date of the case was in 1977.

The last item in our example is the subsequent history of the case. "Rev'd" means that the case was reversed. "444 U.S. 111 (1979)" refers to volume 444 of the United States Reports on page 111. The date of that decision was 1979. As you can see, a lot can be learned about a case just by analyzing its case citation.

I had just begun to grasp the structure of the legal system and how to research a particular topic in the law library when I was asked to write my first paper.

"A good lawyer must be able to write effectively," my Legal Research and Writing teacher told our class. "Now that you have learned how to find the law you must be able to resolve a particular problem in writing."

Before talking about my writing experience, which I'll cover more in chapter 12, I need to shift gears again as the next class on my schedule was Contracts, which met in room C at 10:45 a.m.

CHAPTER 6

Contracts

In this chapter...

- ✓ Briefing a case
- ✓ Sample case brief
- ✓ What is a contract?
- ✓ 4 reasons why cases are included in law textbooks
- ✓ Elements of a valid contract
- ✓ Defenses to breach of contract
- ✓ Remedies for breach of contract
- ✓ Uniform Commercial Code (UCC)

SINCE I ALREADY knew where room C was from my earlier Torts class, I had a fifteen-minute break from my Legal Research and Writing class to either get another cup of coffee or to just gather a few minutes alone to process all my newly acquired information. I chose the latter as I felt jittery enough without the extra caffeine to stimulate my already over-stressed system.

As I took my seat in the lecture hall where my Contracts class was located, I began to see some familiar faces from my previous two classes. The textbook we used for Contracts was Murphy, Speidel and Ayers' casebook, *Studies in Contract Law*. Chapter one dealt with an introduction to the study of contract law. Throughout my first year of this class we studied court cases which illustrated the law governing the conditions and obligations of a contract and the legal remedies available when a contract is breached.

The first case in our textbook, *Bailey v. West*, 22 Ill.340 U.S. 918, 71 S. Ct. 349, 95 L. Ed. 663 (1951), dealt with **mutual assent**. The only problem was that after reading it I still had no idea what mutual assent was or how it related to the law of contracts.

In that case, a race horse was purchased by Richard E. West, the defendant. The horse arrived lame and West had him shipped back to Howard E. Bailey, the original owner. Bailey took care of the horse upon its return to him. Bailey then sued West for his services taking care of the horse. The court concluded that Bailey could not have reasonably believed that West would either authorize or pay for the care of the horse under the factual circumstances of the case. After re-reading this case several times, I gathered that mutual assent means that two or more parties must agree to the reason for the contract.

What is a Contract?

A **contract** is basically a legally enforceable promise. In the *Bailey* case, there was no legally enforceable promise because there was no mutual assent between the parties as to the care of the racehorse. I learned that contract law shows to what extent our society allows people to make promises that are legally binding. For a contract to occur there must be an agreement between two or more persons which creates an obligation to do or not do a particular thing.

The professor then asked the person sitting next to me who the defendant was in the *Bailey* case. You might remember that we talked earlier about the terms appellant and appellee when discussing legal research. However, those terms are used for cases on appeal. The terms **defendant** and **plaintiff** refer to the parties to a lawsuit at the trial court level.

The defendant in the *Bailey* case is West. He is the person who is being sued and who is responding to the complaint. The plaintiff in the *Bailey* case is Bailey, as he is bringing the personal action in court to seek a remedy for an injury to his rights. The plaintiff's name always comes first in the title of the case. In *Bailey*, the plaintiff is seeking to recover the value of his services rendered to the lame racehorse.

I was beginning to see that I was not going to learn the key legal principles of contract law any easier than those of tort law. On my own, I had to distill what mutual assent meant through a thorough analysis of the *Bailey* case.

This revelation of how to find the law through studying cases from our textbook just had me starting to feel good about myself when the professor called upon me to brief the next case, *Hamer v. Sidway*, 124 N.Y. 538, 27 N.E. 256 (N.Y. 1891).

Briefing a Case

In the earlier section about my Torts class we discussed how to use the IRAC approach to analyze case law. That approach is used for law school writing and analysis, law school exams, the bar examination, and the practice of law itself. There is, however, another approach to legal analysis called **case briefing**. You are called upon often by your professors in law school to brief a particular case, so you must always be prepared for class. I saw many of my fellow classmates fall apart when asked questions about a particular case that they had not adequately briefed and prepared for.

A **student brief** is a short summary and analysis of a case; it is a way to sort out the parties, identify the issues, ascertain what was decided, and analyze the reasoning behind why the court decided the way it did. Although these briefs always include the same items of information, the actual way the items are set out can vary, and you should listen to the instructions of your individual professors for how to brief cases for each particular class.

I will show you one way of briefing that worked for me in law school, using the *Hamer v. Sidway* contracts case. The elements of the briefing style I used included:

1. The name of the case;
2. The nature of the case;
3. The facts of the case;
4. The issue;
5. The rule of law or legal rule;

6. The analysis; and

7. The holding or conclusion of the case.

Whatever style you use, you will definitely use your briefs, not only for the classroom discussion, but also for reviewing for exams. Many of my fellow classmates felt that once they were called on in class to brief a case (or dodged a bullet by avoiding being called upon), they were done with their case briefs. The opposite is true. First of all, you may be called upon more than once, as I was that first week of law school. Both my Torts and Contracts professors called upon me on the same day.

The other reason briefs are so important is that they form the basis of your outline for your exams and are helpful tools for spotting issues and applying legal rules.

Now, let's go over a contracts case using a **student brief**.

If you are writing your brief down on a separate sheet of paper (and I suggest that you do so for your first year of law school), you would write the case name and page number from the textbook at the top of the page. Some students brief the case directly in their books. This may save time in the short term, but it is harder to go back through all the cases in your book come exam time. It is more efficient to have your briefs all laid out on separate sheets of paper. You can also type your brief on your laptop.

The **name of the case** I was asked to brief was *Hamer v. Sidway*. The next element of my brief was the **nature of the case**. This identifies the **form of action** (e.g., negligence, breach of contract, assault), the **type of proceeding** (e.g., appeal from summary judgment, demurrer), and the **relief sought** (e.g., injunction, criminal sanctions, monetary damages). In other words, the nature of the case is a brief statement of the legal character and procedural status of a case. The key to figuring out the nature of the case is to decide who is asking the court for what. For those of you who don't know, a **summary judgment** is one party's effort to put an early end to a lawsuit when he or she believes that there are no important facts in dispute. A **demurrer** is a written response to a complaint filed in a lawsuit which, in essence, asks for a dismissal because, even if the facts in the complaint were true, there is no legal basis for a lawsuit. In *Hamer*, I told the professor that the nature of the case was an action on appeal to recover for a contract based on forbearance of a right as a consideration. Thus, the form of action was for breach of contract and the type of proceeding was an appeal from a trial court judgment. The relief sought was monetary.

In *Hamer*, the lawsuit was brought by the assignee of the nephew, William Story II, against the executor of the estate of the decedent, William Story I.

Does the above sound confusing? Let me tell you that it is, and that only by having a brief where you can fit all the pieces of the puzzle together does it make sense. Contractual relationships are varied and complex.

A lot of terminology I was unfamiliar with popped up in this case. Let me start with **assignee**. In the law, a person can assign or transfer his or her interest in property, contract or other rights to another. In *Hamer*, the nephew, William Story

II, transferred his $5,000 from the above contract to another person. That person is the assignee.

An **executor** is a person who is appointed to carry out the terms of the will of a deceased person (often referred to as the **decedent**).

Sometimes the language in the cases you read in law school, and even later when practicing law, can be daunting to say the least. However, law school is set up the way it is to teach you how to look up the right cases while practicing law and sift quickly through the details to discover any pertinent information needed.

The next item in my brief was the **facts of the case**. This is a brief factual summary designed to refresh your memory should your professor call upon you. In *Hamer*, William Story I promised to pay his nephew, William Story II, $5,000 if he refrained from drinking liquor, using tobacco, swearing, and playing cards or billiards for money until he was 21 years old. Meanwhile William Story II's uncle died, and the younger William Story had transferred his right to the $5,000 to another person. He, indeed, kept his part of the bargain, although the executor of William Story I stated that the nephew never promised anything in return for the money and refused to pay it to the assignee.

This brings us to the next part of my legal brief—the **issue**. We spoke about the issue earlier in our discussion of my torts class and the IRAC approach. To reiterate, the issue of a case is a general statement of the legal question illustrated in the case. To make it simple, the issue is the rule of law put in the form of a "yes or no" type of question. In *Hamer*, the rule of law was

that **forbearance** (refraining from the enforcement of something, such as a debt, right, or obligation, that is due) is valuable
consideration. Hence, the issue would be whether forbearance
is sufficient consideration for a valid contract. In essence, the
issue deals with what is in dispute.

Let's move on to the fourth element of briefing a case, the
concise rule of law or **legal rule,** which the court was applying
in a particular case. This is a statement of the general principle
of law that the case illustrates. In *Hamer*, the legal rule is that
forbearance of a right is a valuable consideration. When I told
that to the professor I was reading it right out of the casebook
and didn't really understand what it meant. Thank goodness she
didn't question me at that time. Actually, all that the above legal
rule means is that if one gives up something that is bargained
for, that act of forbearance constitutes consideration.

Consideration is one of the elements necessary for a valid
contract to exist. Consideration is the **inducement** to a contract.
In the law of contracts, the inducement is a pledge or promise
that causes individuals to enter into an agreement. Often you
will see the Latin term *quid pro quo* used when referring to the
consideration for a contract. *Quid pro quo* means "this for that."
There must be a bargained-for exchange.

The **analysis** comes next in a student brief. In terms of the
Hamer case, William Story I promised $5,000 plus interest to
his nephew, William Story II, for his promise to refrain from
drinking liquor, using tobacco, swearing and playing cards or
billiards for money until he was 21 years old. After William
Story II celebrated his 21st birthday, he wrote to his uncle and

requested the promised $5,000. The two subsequently agreed through written correspondence that William Story II would allow William Story I to keep the money, allowing it to accrue interest, until William Story II became older.

William Story I died without having transferred the money to his nephew as agreed. In the meantime, William Story II had transferred the $5,000 financial interest to his wife, who later still had transferred this financial interest to Louisa Hamer. After William Story I died, the executor of William Story I's estate, Franklin Sidway, refused to pay the promised $5,000 to Ms. Hamer. Since the rule of law is that forbearance is valuable consideration, and William Story II indeed gave up drinking liquor, using tobacco, swearing and playing cards or billiards for money until he was 21 years old, consideration did indeed exist between the parties.

That brings us to the **holding** and **decision**, or the **conclusion,** of the case. In *Hamer*, the court concluded that forbearance of a right is valuable consideration. The holding contains a discussion of the rule of the case and the court's rationale at arriving at its decision. The **rationale** is the reason the court decided the case the way it did.

The court, in *Hamer*, held that valuable consideration exists if one party benefits and the other party suffers some forbearance, detriment or loss. On an aside, the modern way of teaching contract law is that a contract is a bargained for exchange which doesn't require a detriment. In other words, something of value doesn't necessarily need to be given in return for performance or promise of performance in a contract.

4 Reasons Why Cases are Included in Law Textbooks

You should also be prepared to answer the professor should he or she ask you why the case was included in your textbook. There are four major reasons why a particular case merits inclusion in your casebook.

The first is for the **majority rule.** As we discussed in Legal Research and Writing earlier on in my diary, the majority ruling is the opinion of the majority of the justices or judges in a particular case. The majority ruling in an appellate court case essentially becomes the law. Thus, a case may be included in the casebook for the decision of the majority of the court.

A case may also be included in your textbook for the **minority or dissenting opinion**. This is written by a judge or justice who disagrees with the majority opinion. Often this opinion contains information (called *dicta*) which could prove to be a valuable tool for you to explain and weigh competing policies while writing office memos and as you argue for the social good your future clients will ostensibly seek. In law school and beyond, you will be constantly examining the cases you read for the value choices supporting the legal rules contained in the decisions. When values or beliefs change in society, legal change will often follow.

The next reason a case may be included in your textbook is for **historical significance**, such as the anonymous case dated 1466 I discussed in the Torts portion of my diary.

Lastly, a case may be included in your casebook because it was **decided wrong**. All of these reasons are important to understand, not only to answer questions posed to you by your law professors, but also to understand the significance of the particular cases you may be researching as an attorney representing a client.

Thus, by briefing a case you are on your way to understanding what the law is all about, namely to look at the law as a series of rules and policies for regulating our behavior in society. Case law makes the rules, while social policies are the underlying values or purposes behind the rules.

If briefing a case sounds overwhelming, don't despair. Your first year of law school is no easy task; however, if you use the format in Table 6.1 consistently, you will eventually be able to quickly read a case while searching for the relevant information you need. This sample case brief is available for download at www.abclawschooldiary.com. Briefs are invaluable for classroom reference, as well as for exam review. You will learn through repetition how to go over a particular legal concept and apply it to other factual settings besides the case it came from. This is an important tool as law school exams contain factual situations you will be asked to analyze using the relevant rule of law.

SAMPLE CASE BRIEF

1. Case Name

_____ v. _____
(petitioner)   (respondent)

2. Nature of the Case/Procedural Background
Date of decision (in highest court) _____

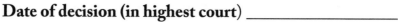

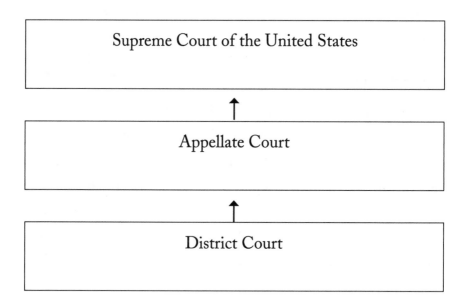

Supreme Court of the United States

↑

Appellate Court

↑

District Court

3. Facts of the Case _____

_____

_____

_____

_____

4. Legal Issue _____

_____

_____

5. Rule of Law _____

_____

_____

6. Analysis _____

_____

_____

7. Holding or Decision

Note the following vocabulary:

Affirmed = The appellate court agrees with the opinion of the lower court

Reversed = The appellate court disagrees with the opinion of the lower court

Remanded = The case is sent back to the court from which it came for further action

_____

_____

_____

Table 6.1

Elements of a Valid Contract

Before we move onto the next class, I would like to end my discussion of contract law by going over the elements of a valid contract. Bear in mind that we spent an entire year developing these elements in detail. You won't be responsible for all of these concepts from the get-go. However, it will help to have reviewed them before your first day of Contract Law.

The elements of a valid contract are:

1. Offer;
2. Acceptance;
3. Consideration in the form of money or a promise to do or not do something;
4. Mutuality between parties to carry out the promises of the contract; and
5. Certainty of terms.

The first element of a valid contract is the **offer**. An offer can be made by a written document, orally or by the conduct of the parties.

The second element of a valid contract is **acceptance**. The offer must be accepted in order to form a contract. I was taught contract law in terms of offer and acceptance. However, the modern approach has more to do with mutual assent, which is the applied words and conduct of the parties.

The third element of a valid contract is **consideration**, which we previously discussed in connection with the *Hamer* case. As I stated earlier, consideration is the inducement to a contract. There must be a bargained for exchange for a valid contract to exist.

The fourth element of a valid contract is **mutuality.** This concept is closely related to that of consideration. Both parties must be bound to perform their obligations under the contract or the law will bind neither one to perform the agreement.

The fifth element of a valid contract is **certainty**. The terms of the contract must be sufficiently definite.

The above abbreviated version of the elements of a valid contract form the mainstay of contract law, and if you can understand them you are well on your way to deciphering the realm of contracts. I, on the other hand, had to discern these principles through reading and briefing the cases in my Contracts textbook.

Defenses to Breach of Contract

In addition, you will learn the defenses for defendants who are sued for breach of contract. Here is a list of the defenses which we studied in depth during the entire first year of contract law:

1. **Legality** (If a contract is illegal and there is equal fault in both parties, the court will generally not enforce the contract);
2. **Statute of frauds** (A *statute* requiring certain contracts to be in writing and signed by the parties bound by the contract);
3. **Capacity** (e.g., the defendant was incompetent, insane or intoxicated when the contract was created);

4. **Unconscionability** (extreme unfairness by an objective standard);
5. **Mistake**;
6. **Fraud**;
7. **Undue influence**; and
8. **Duress**.

Again, this list of defenses to the duty to perform a contract is what I was taught during my first year of law school. Many of these concepts may be taught in a different manner, depending on where you go to law school. I just want you to become familiar with the overall picture of the realm of contract law.

Remedies for Breach of Contract

We also studied in depth the remedies available to compensate the plaintiff for breach of contract, which include **damages** (puts the plaintiff in a position that he or she would have been in had the contract been performed), **restitution** (restores to the plaintiff the value of a benefit that was unjustly conferred, regardless of contract price), and **specific performance** (breaching party is ordered to carry out the contract duties *or* is enjoined from action.)

Uniform Commercial Code

Lastly, we studied in depth the **Uniform Commercial Code** (UCC) during our year-long course. Contract law is governed by the common law (the part of English law which is derived from custom and judicial precedent, rather than statutes) and the UCC. Contractual transactions involving real estate, services, insurance, intangible assets and employment are governed by the common law, while contractual transactions involving goods and tangible objects (such as purchasing a car) are governed by the UCC. The common law and UCC have distinct differences, and we spent a lot of time going over these two bodies of contract law.

There is definitely a method to the madness of your first year of law school. Without going through the arduous process of briefing an endless array of cases, you would not be equipped to deal with the practice of law upon graduation and passing the bar examination.

Law school is set up the way that it is to prepare you for your career as an attorney. Of course, I didn't understand that concept at the time. All I could think was how I would be able to adequately read and brief the cases for each of my classes. I was in survival mode, but you don't have to be.

My aim is to help you understand the broader picture so that your first year law experience has a deeper meaning than just meeting short-term goals. Let's move onto a discussion of Civil Procedure, the next class on my first year schedule.

CHAPTER 7

Civil Procedure

In this chapter...

- ✓ The federal court system
- ✓ State and territorial court systems
- ✓ Personal jurisdiction
- ✓ Evolution of personal jurisdiction over nonresident defendants
- ✓ Other types of jurisdiction
- ✓ Diversity jurisdiction
- ✓ Venue
- ✓ Pleadings and discovery

SINCE I DID not know any of my fellow classmates very well (after all it was only my first official day of school), I chose to drive off campus for a quick bite to eat. I probably should have swallowed my pride and asked one of my fellow classmates to accompany me. I could have used a friend to discuss the three classes I had already attended and to just plain commiserate with.

However, instead I chose to dine alone and wallow in my own fears and expectations. I arrived back on campus in plenty of time to find my way to my 1:15 p.m. Civil Procedure class.

I had no idea whatsoever what Civil Procedure was all about. I could grasp what a contract and a tort was, but what did civil procedure have to do with the law? Contracts and torts deal with what lawyers do in civil court, while civil procedure deals with the complex rules that govern courtroom trials and often the steps preceding them, such as discovery, pleadings, etc. In other words, you will learn in Civil Procedure the various methods or procedures through which courts decide a particular case.

Before I delve into my first day of class, I'd like to spend some time discussing the United States court system. We talked about this briefly in the section on Legal Research and Writing, and I wanted to go over it again here as it will make Civil Procedure easier to understand. There are two separate court systems in the United States, the **federal court system** and the **state and territorial court systems**.

The Federal Court System

The federal court system is made up of four levels of courts. **The federal courts and other entities** handle military tribunals (Courts Martial), the United States Tax Court, the Court of Appeals for Veteran Claims, and a number of federal administrative agencies and boards.

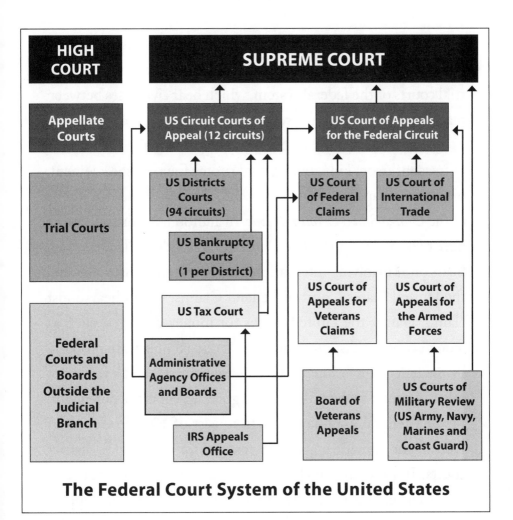

The Federal Court System of the United States

Table 7.1

The federal trial courts consist of 94 U.S. district courts which are organized into 13 districts. The district courts are the trial courts of the federal system, which hear civil cases between plaintiffs and defendants from two or more states or territories, as well as bankruptcy cases. They also hear criminal cases such as treason, arson, kidnapping, bankruptcy fraud, embezzlement, biological weapons, and other federal crimes as listed in Title 18 of the *United States Criminal Code*. In addition, the district courts have two special courts: The Court of International Trade, which hears cases involving international trade and customs issues, and the United States Court of Federal Claims, which hears most claims against the United States for money damages, such as federal contract disputes, unlawful "takings" of private property by the federal government, vaccine injury cases, and a variety of other matters in which the federal government is the defendant.

The **federal appellate courts** consist of 13 U.S. Courts of Appeal and provide appellate oversight for the 13 U.S. district courts. If a plaintiff or defendant in a U.S. district court feels that their case was handled inappropriately, they may appeal the court decision in the U.S. Court of Appeal for the district in which their original case was tried.

The **United States Supreme Court** is the highest court in the land and the absolute final court of appeal for any court case, whether state or federal. The Supreme Court is made up of the Chief Justice of the United States and eight associate justices, who are nominated by the President of the United States and confirmed by Congress. The Supreme Court has original jurisdiction (meaning the Court actually tries a case) over certain types of cases, such as suits between two or more states and/or cases involving ambassadors and other public ministers.

The Supreme Court is perhaps more well-known for the cases it hears on appeal from the U.S. Courts of Appeals, as well as from the various state supreme courts. It is not possible for the Court to hear every case sent to them on appeal from the lower courts. The Court receives about 10,000 petitions for a **writ of certiorari**, the instrument the Court uses to request documents from the lower courts for cases they decide to hear. The Supreme Court, at its discretion, hears only around 100 to 150 cases each year. Those cases are usually selected either because the lower courts have differed on a legal issue or ruled in such a way that it contravened previous Supreme Court rulings, or because the case involves important questions about the Constitution or federal law.

Let's now move on to a brief discussion of the **state and territorial court systems** before delving into my first day of Civil Procedure.

State and Territorial Court Systems

Each state and territory of the United States has its own system of courts. State court systems mirror the federal court system in terms of organization and function, but they operate entirely independently of the federal system. The only time cases tried and appealed in state courts cross over into the federal system is if a case reviewed by a state supreme court is appealed to the United States Supreme Court.

The state courts are courts of **general jurisdiction** and they hear all of the cases not selected for federal courts. In our dual court system, the federal courts interpret and enforce federal laws, whereas the state courts interpret and enforce state laws. Because each of the states has developed differently and has a different history from the others, each state has also developed different laws. Indeed, prior to the Civil War, each state more or less considered itself a separate sovereign entity. Because the states operate somewhat autonomously, with different geography and population needs, the state courts are organized somewhat differently as well. However, they share similar structures and processes.

As with the federal courts, cases in the state courts start in the lower courts, or the **trial courts**. The names for the various trial courts in each state may differ slightly, but there is a general uniformity of functions the lower courts handle. From probate to family matters such as divorce and child custody hearings, to traffic court, civil trials and criminal trials, the state courts handle the everyday business of enforcing state laws and assist their citizens in obtaining justice in their day to day lives. In normal practice, most lawyers are predominantly reliant on state law.

You might well ask what the above has to do with civil procedure? The answer is two-fold. With the complicated court and law enforcement system that we have, if we didn't standardize legal procedure to some degree our society would be a land of total chaos. Secondly, one of the main areas of law explored by civil procedure is **jurisdiction,** which is the power to hear and determine a case. In other words, before a court can consider a case it must have the power to hear and decide the outcome of that case. Without jurisdiction a court has no authority over a case.

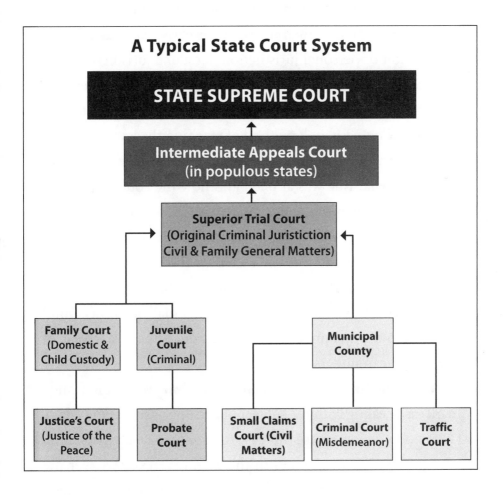

Table 7.2

Personal Jurisdiction

Our textbook for Civil Procedure started out with cases dealing with the evolution of **personal jurisdiction**. This class turned out to be no different than my previous classes in that a simple explanation of personal jurisdiction, let alone jurisdiction, was nowhere to be found. Once again it was up to the students to find the answers using the process of briefing the cases to find their way. This casebook method of teaching the law (expecting the law student to analyze the language of the case in order to figure out what rule was applied and how the court applied it) was becoming more and more apparent to me as the day wore on!

I was relieved when I was *not* called upon to brief a case that day. I actually enjoyed watching a fellow classmate squirm as he was asked to brief the case of *Pennoyer v. Neff,* 95 U.S. 714, 5 Otto 714, 24 L. Ed. 565 (1878). Not in a malicious way, mind you, but in a way only those going through their first year of law school can understand.

We spent quite a bit of time studying *Pennoyer* as it is a landmark case dealing with the subject of personal jurisdiction. Many law schools no longer use this case to show personal jurisdiction, as many significant changes in this area have evolved over the past several years. The date of the *Pennoyer* case was 1878, an instant clue that the case was in our textbook because of its historical significance. The Court held that personal jurisdiction is acquired by personal service inside the territorial limits of the **forum state** (the state where the lawsuit is brought) as well as by voluntary appearance of the defendant in the forum state to contest the suit on its merits.

What does the above really mean? First of all, the plaintiff's goal when suing a defendant is to do so in the court most convenient and favorable to the plaintiff. Thus, the forum chosen is usually a court in the plaintiff's home state. Personal jurisdiction deals with the power of the court to bring all of the parties before it and to render a binding judgment upon the parties. ***In personam* jurisdiction** stands for "over the person." In the *Pennoyer* case the Court was dealing with obtaining personal jurisdiction over a nonresident defendant.

Let's use a hypothetical example to illustrate *in personam* jurisdiction and how a different set of facts can illustrate the rule of law in the *Pennoyer* case. Pretend that a plaintiff, Mr. Blue, sues a defendant, Mr. Green, for breach of contract. The contract took place in California where Mr. Blue lives. However, Mr. Green lives in Utah. The question becomes one of how Mr. Blue can successfully sue Mr. Green in California, since a court must have the proper authority to hear a particular case.

The rule of law in the *Pennoyer* case states that personal jurisdiction can occur in one of two ways: personal service within the state, or voluntary appearance in court by the defendant to contest the lawsuit. **Personal service** (or **service of process**) is the delivery of legal notice to a party in a case. Any party who is being sued is entitled to advance notice of the suit. Notice consists of a copy of the complaint and a summons to appear in court.

Applying the above to our set of facts, we would deduce that if the defendant, Mr. Green, is either personally served notice of the suit while in California or if he comes to California to defend the suit, the court will have the personal jurisdiction necessary to hear the case.

Mr. Green might make a **special appearance** in California to challenge the court's ability to assert jurisdiction over him. This type of procedure means that the defendant would only argue against jurisdiction, and thus NOT subject himself to jurisdiction over the merits of the case.

If, however, Mr. Green makes a **general appearance** in California, he would submit himself to the court's jurisdiction by defending the case on the merits without being able to object to jurisdiction. Appearances are further complicated in today's world where video conferencing between the judge, plaintiff and defendant are becoming more common.

If the defendant in our example were to make either a special or general appearance before the California courts, he would be making a **direct attack**. A direct attack on a judicial proceeding is an attempt to avoid or correct it in some manner provided by law; in our discussion of civil procedure this occurs when a defendant enters a case and moves to dismiss it for lack of jurisdiction. A direct attack differs from a **collateral attack,** whereby a defendant does not enter the case and allows a **default judgment** to be entered against him. (For those of you who don't know, a default judgment occurs when the defendant has not responded to a summons or has failed to appear before a court of law. The *default* is the failure on the part of the defendant to act.) After the judgment is made in favor of the plaintiff, the defendant would then make an appearance claiming improper jurisdiction. In other words, a collateral attack is an attack on a prior judgment in a new case

Just as I thought I was understanding what personal jurisdiction was, I was dismayed to find out that the inclusion of not only the *Pennoyer* case, but also the next three cases we studied in our casebook were only there for their historical significance. Personal jurisdiction went through quite an evolution with cases ranging from 1878 (*Pennoyer v. Neff*) to 1980 (*World-Wide Volkswagen Corp. v. Woodson*).

Evolution of Personal Jurisdiction over Nonresident Defendants

In the series of cases we studied, the Supreme Court repeatedly defined the limitations of the Fourteenth Amendment Due Process Clause on the exercise of personal jurisdiction over nonresident defendants. For example, we studied the case of *Hess v. Pawloski*, 274 U.S. 352 (1927), which dealt with nonresident motorist statutes and the exercise of state police power to enforce them. Further, in *Blackmer v. United States*, 284 U.S. 421 (1932), the Supreme Court held that personal jurisdiction may be based upon U.S. citizenship, and in *Miliken v. Meyer*, 311 U.S. 457 (1940), the Court stated that personal jurisdiction may be based upon the defendant's domicile within the forum state. **Domicile** refers to an individual's permanent home as opposed to a temporary or periodic residence. A person can have many transient residences but only one legal domicile, which is the home address to which he always intends to return for prolonged periods.

In my Civil Procedure class, we studied the above cases in depth, as well as the infamous *International Shoe Co. v. Washington*, 326 U.S. 310 (1945). This case is the foundation for studying and analyzing modern personal jurisdiction issues. In *International Shoe* the law of **minimum contacts** was coined. Minimum contacts basically means that a party, particularly a corporation, must have enough contacts in a state other than the one he or she (or it) resides in so as to avoid unfairness and injustice if sued in that other state. This ruling has had a significant effect on corporations involved in interstate commerce.

In *Hanson v. Denckla*, 357 U.S. 235 (1958) the Supreme Court went even further to define personal jurisdiction to include the **purposeful availment** requirement. The Court stated that "it is essential in each case that there be some act by which the defendant purposefully avails itself of the privilege of conducting activities within the forum state, thus involving the benefits and protections of its laws." This decision addressed the question of whether the probate court in one state or the **trustee** (the person who is legally assigned to administer the trust) in another state had jurisdiction over the trust.

During the period from 1945 to 1980, the states began to enact **long arm statutes**. In other words, taking our above example involving Mr. Green, if he has minimum contacts within California, the long arm of the California law can reach into Utah to serve him a summons and complaint, forcing him to appear before the California court and be subject to its jurisdiction.

In 1980, *World-Wide Volkswagen Corp. v. Woodson*, **444 U.S. 286** (1980) began the **stream of commerce** analysis in defective product litigation and defined where a defendant can anticipate or foresee being hauled into court in a venue that is *fairer* to the plaintiff than the defendant. Each Supreme Court case from *Pennoyer* to *World-Wide Volkswagen Corp* provided some part of the collection of the rules of law applicable to the personal jurisdiction issues I studied during my first year of Civil Procedure. Throughout the course of this class we also learned the appropriate rules contained in the federal rules of civil procedure concerning the sources of personal jurisdiction in federal court.

If the above discussion of personal jurisdiction seems confounding, don't be disheartened. It was for me as well; however, we spent a good part of my first semester studying the above concepts of which I briefly scratched the surface. It is likely that personal jurisdiction will continue to be an issue the Supreme Court will revisit periodically as changes in our society and new challenges to the concept occur. For example, the current decade has seen three new cases involving this topic: *BNSF Railway Co. v. Tyrrell*, 137 S.Ct. 810 (2017), *Bristol-Myers Squibb Co. v. Superior Court of California*, 137 S.Ct. 1773 (2017), and *Daimler AG v. Bauman*, 134 S. Ct. 746 (2014). Although I did not study these cases, I wanted to include a reference to them to demonstrate the continuing refinement of this concept in the court system, showing a trend to renew the traditional notions of fair play and substantial justice, and to reinforce the long-standing principles which underly personal jurisdiction.

Other Types of Jurisdiction

Personal jurisdiction was but one of the many aspects of civil procedure we studied. In closing my discussion of this topic, I want to familiarize you with the other types of jurisdiction which were covered in length during my first year Civil Procedure course.

1. **Jurisdiction over property:** There are two types of jurisdiction over property. The first one is **_in rem_ jurisdiction,** which refers to jurisdiction over a thing in controversy. The second type is **_quasi in rem_ jurisdiction**, which refers to the court's power to attach property in order to obtain jurisdiction over a person. However, the U.S. Supreme Court largely abolished the exercise of _quasi in rem_ jurisdiction in _Shaffer v. Heitner_, 433 US 186 (1977), except in exceptional circumstances that might arise while dealing with real property, such as land, and when the owner of land cannot be found.

2. **Subject matter jurisdiction:** This type of jurisdiction refers to the restriction on the types of cases a court can hear. **Limited jurisdiction** exists when a court

is limited to a specific subject matter such as probate and divorce. **General jurisdiction** exists when a court can hear any type of case.

3. **Original jurisdiction:** This type of jurisdiction governs the trial courts. These courts have the authority to hear the case first.

4. **Appellate jurisdiction:** This type of jurisdiction exists with the appellate courts whose job it is to review the record of the trial courts.

5. **Federal jurisdiction:** This type of jurisdiction arises in several types of cases enumerated under Article III of the United States Constitution, or in which there is a federal statute granting jurisdiction. In other words, the federal courts have **limited jurisdiction** to hear specific types of cases, while the state courts have **general jurisdiction**. State courts can hear almost any type of case.

6. **Concurrent jurisdiction:** This type of jurisdiction arises when two different courts have authority to hear the same case.

7. **Exclusive jurisdiction:** This type of jurisdiction arises when only one court has the authority to hear a particular case.

We spent an extensive amount of time going over the various types of jurisdiction through studying the cases in our Civil Procedure textbook

Diversity Jurisdiction

At this point I want to briefly familiarize you with the **Erie doctrine,** which mandates that federal courts in diversity jurisdiction cases apply the substantive law of the state in which they sit. **Diversity jurisdiction** (28 U.S. Code § 1332) is a federal court's power to hear any case where the amount in controversy exceeds $75,000 and no plaintiff shares a state of citizenship with any defendant.

The U.S. Supreme Court's decision in *Erie R.R. v. Tompkins*, 304 U.S. 64 (1938), established the **substance versus procedure test** for diversity actions. An issue that clearly addresses legal rights is substantive and is to be resolved according to state law, while issues that clearly pertain to the judicial process alone are procedural and invoke federal law. Do you remember we talked about the difference between substantive law and procedural law in the section on Legal Research and Writing?

To review, substantive law is the body of laws that structure and govern the members of our society, while procedural law is the set of procedures used for making, administering, and enforcing substantive law. Hopefully, you are beginning to see how interconnected all of these core classes are.

Venue

Besides studying jurisdiction in depth during this course, we also studied **venue**. Venue, as opposed to jurisdiction, involves the particular geographic area within a judicial district where a suit should be brought. Venue deals with trying a lawsuit in a district where the interests of justice, as well as the convenience of the parties and witnesses, are considered.

Pleadings and Discovery

It became clear to me, as we progressed from the study of jurisdiction and venue to the study of pleadings, just how important civil procedure is in terms of trying a lawsuit. Without a proper knowledge of the paperwork involved in litigation how could one ever learn the skills and processes necessary to practice as an attorney? Some of the things an attorney deals with on a habitual basis are pleadings and discovery.

A **pleading** is a formal written statement of one party's claims or defenses to another party's claims in a civil action. In other words, pleadings state the basic positions of the parties in a lawsuit. Common pre-trial pleadings include the **complaint, answer, reply, and counterclaim**. The most important pleading in a civil case is the complaint, which sets out the plaintiff's version of the facts and specifies the damages. A complaint frames the issues of a case.

The actual facts surrounding an action come to light through the use of **discovery**. Discovery is a pre-trial procedure in which the parties to a lawsuit can obtain evidence from the other party through the use of devices such as a **request for answers to interrogatories, request for production of documents**, and **request for admissions and depositions**. In addition, we studied **verdicts** and **judgments,** as well as rules for a trial and post-trial.

As you can see, Civil Procedure is a hands-on course dealing with the entire scope of litigation in the court system. Let's move on now to a discussion of Criminal Law and Procedure, which deals with offenses against the state, as opposed to civil cases which are usually disputes between individuals and adjudicated through civil lawsuits.

CHAPTER 8

Criminal Law and Procedure

In this chapter...

- ✓ Substantive vs. procedural criminal law
- ✓ *Actus reus* and *mens rea*
- ✓ Felonies and misdemeanors
- ✓ Categories of crimes
- ✓ Defenses to crimes
- ✓ Differences between civil and criminal law
- ✓ Criminal procedure constitutional safeguards
- ✓ Sixth Amendment right to counsel
- ✓ Fourth Amendment protection against unreasonable searches and seizures
- ✓ Federal exclusionary rule
- ✓ Essay exam writing tips

ONCE MY CIVIL Procedure class was over at 2:15 p.m., I was done for the day. And what a day it had been!! Instead of resting on my laurels, I headed home to study for my classes the following day. Besides having Civil Procedure once again the following day, Tuesday, I also had two new classes to contend with—Real Property Law and Criminal Law.

Unfortunately, 9:30 a.m. rolled around too quickly for my taste on Tuesday morning, but I took my seat in the infamous classroom C for my Criminal Law class.

Our textbook devoted the first ninety-eight pages to the concept of the **criminal justice system**. The criminal justice system basically enforces the standards of conduct that a community considers important and necessary.

Substantive vs Procedural Criminal Law

There are two types of criminal law in the United States criminal justice system: substantive and procedural. **Substantive criminal law** defines what conduct is criminal and prescribes the punishment to be imposed for such conduct. Both the concepts of criminal conduct and punishment were thoroughly examined during our semester of Criminal Law. **Procedural criminal law** consists of the procedures used to investigate and prosecute criminal behavior. We studied Criminal Procedure during our second semester and I will discuss that portion of criminal law later on. Substantive criminal law has a long history and can be traced back thousands of years in Western society.

Actus Reus and Mens Rea

In our modern criminal law system, there are a number of crimes and punishments that our society imposes on community offenders; before I discuss these, however, I would like to talk about two important concepts you should be familiar with: **actus reus** and **mens rea**. These are the foundations for criminal law, so I want to make sure you understand these topics, as they will come up on essays, exams, and on the bar examination as well. In keeping with my other classes, our professor naturally relied heavily on Socratic dialogue to teach us about *actus reus* and *mens rea*.

Simply stated, for behavior to be punishable, a person must commit an overt criminal act called an **actus reus**, or a "guilty act," and have a culpable intent, known as **mens rea**, or "guilty mind."

We discussed *mens rea*, or intent, in *State v. Rocker*, 475 P.2d 684 (Haw., 1970), which was contained in our textbook. Luckily, I was not called upon to discuss this case, even though I had diligently briefed it the night before using the method that I discussed with you in the section on contracts. I listened as the student sitting on my left explained the facts of the case to the professor. She stated that the defendants, Richard Barry Rocker and Joseph Cava, openly sunbathed in the nude at a public beach and were charged with creating a common nuisance. The issue in the case was whether one must intend an act to be criminal to be charged with creating a common nuisance. The Court held that one need only have a general intent, or intent to commit acts one knows are likely to be seen by others as guilty of creating a public nuisance.

On an aside, a **public nuisance** includes a variety of minor crimes that threaten the health, morals, safety, comfort, convenience, or welfare of a community, as opposed to the injury being suffered by an individual. However, this case was not in our textbook to talk about the crime of a public nuisance; instead we studied it to learn about *mens rea*. There must be a specific state of mind on the part of the defendant to hold him or her criminally liable.

We fleshed out the concept of the mental state referred to as *mens rea* during the course of our semester of Criminal Law. There are many more nuances, but I just want to familiarize you here with the basics of this important component of criminal law. To summarize, for an act to be a crime, the person committing it must *intend* to do something that the state legislature or Congress has determined to be a wrong. There must be *criminal intent*.

This concept is based on the belief in our legal system that people should be punished only when they have acted in a way that makes them morally blameworthy; intentionally engaging in behavior prohibited by the law. However, I want to point out that there are some crimes that do *not* require *mens rea*. These are **strict liability laws** which are enacted because the social benefits of strict enforcement outweigh the harm of punishing a person who may be morally innocent. Two examples of such laws are:

1. Statutory rape laws
2. Sale of alcohol to minor laws.

In addition to the mental state of the accused (***mens rea***) there must also be ***actus reus,*** which is an action or conduct that is an element of a crime. For the rest of the semester we studied these concepts in the context of various crimes. A crime is a wrong or offense against society. In every state, crimes are put into categories which are usually categorized as **felonies, misdemeanors,** or **infractions**. Decisions on crime classifications are made by state legislators.

Infractions (also called violations) are petty offenses that are typically punishable by fines and not jail time. In my first year Criminal Law class, we spent a great deal of time learning about the other two classifications of crimes: felonies, and misdemeanors.

Felonies and Misdemeanors

The main distinction between a **felony** and a **misdemeanor** is that the punishment for felonies can be death or imprisonment in a federal or state penitentiary for more than one year, while a misdemeanor is defined as a crime punishable by a fine, probation, community service, restitution, or confinement up to one year in most states. A felony, like a misdemeanor conviction, may not result in time behind bars, but due to being the most serious type of criminal offense there is a greater potential for imprisonment, ranging from time in prison (a year is often the low end), to life in prison without parole or even death.

We covered several types of felonies including **homicide** (the killing of one human being by another; examples are murder and manslaughter), **robbery, rape, burglary, grand larceny, bribery,** and **arson.** Each one of these felonies has specific elements that must be met before a defendant can be found guilty. I just want you to become familiar with the broad picture for now.

In terms of misdemeanors, we covered **public intoxication, vagrancy, prostitution, petit larceny, disturbing the peace**, and **assault and battery**.

Categories of Crimes

The following four categories of crimes will help you to get a broad overview of criminal law:

1. **Personal Crimes:** These are crimes which result in physical or mental harm to another individual.
   a. Assault;
   b. Battery;
   c. False Imprisonment;
   d. Kidnapping; and
   e. Homicide;
      - First and second-degree murder;
      - Involuntary manslaughter; and
      - Vehicular homicide.
   f. Rape, statutory rape, sexual assault, and other sexual offenses.
2. **Property Crimes:** These crimes involve interfering with another's right to use or enjoy their property.
   a. Larceny (theft);
   b. Robbery (theft by force);
   c. Burglary;
   d. Arson;

    e. Embezzlement;

    f. Forgery;

    g. False pretenses; and

    h. Receipt of stolen goods.

3. **Inchoate Crimes:** These are crimes that are *incomplete*. In other words, they were begun but not completed. The defendant must have taken a substantial step to complete the crime.

    a. Any crime where there is attempt, such as "attempted burglary;"

    b. Solicitation; and

    c. Conspiracy.

4. **Statutory Crimes**: These are violations of state or federal statutes.

    a. Alcohol-related crimes; and

    b. Selling alcohol to a minor.

Defenses to Crimes

Lastly, our Criminal Law class went over in detail the defenses to a crime such as insanity, intoxication, infancy, justifiable use of force, duress, and other defenses. In addition, these issues of criminal law can be found on your law school tests, essays, and the bar examination. For example, on the 2006 bar examination, there was a full Criminal Law essay where the examiners tested students on first degree murder, second degree murder, voluntary manslaughter, and insanity.

Differences Between Civil and Criminal Law

At this point, I'd like to discuss some relevant differences between present day civil and criminal law in the United States. The American legal system is made up of two very different types of cases: civil and criminal ones. Crimes are generally offenses against the state, and are accordingly prosecuted by the state, as opposed to civil cases, which are usually disputes between individuals and adjudicated through civil lawsuits.

In **civil law** (the law of torts and contracts, for example), there is an injured party called the plaintiff, while in criminal law the injured party is either the people of the state or the United States. As we discussed earlier in the section on Civil Procedure, there are two court systems in the United States: **federal** and **state** courts. In the federal system, whether it is a criminal or civil trial, the jury must reach a *unanimous* verdict. This is in contrast to state courts, where whether a jury needs to be unanimous depends on the state and type of trial. For criminal cases, nearly every state requires the jury to have a unanimous verdict. For civil cases, almost 1/3 of states require only a majority for a verdict, while some states require a majority if the money at issue on trial is below a certain amount, and a unanimous verdict at all other times.

A third difference has to do with the pleas in a criminal case versus a civil case. In a civil case, the defendant is found to be **liable** or **not liable** for the alleged wrong. If the defendant is found to be liable, then there is a money judgment in favor of the plaintiff that is paid by the defendant. In addition to, or in place of, monetary damages, **injunctive relief** may be sought in a civil lawsuit; this is basically a court order for the defendant to stop a specified act or behavior.

In criminal law, a defendant is held to be either **guilty** or **not guilty** of the crime with which he or she is charged. A plea of not guilty requires that the other side must prove the defendant's guilt **beyond a reasonable doubt**. In criminal law, a defendant is either fined, imprisoned, or placed on probation.

There is another option for the criminal defendant besides pleading guilty or not guilty. The defendant can ask the judge to accept a plea of **nolo contendere**, or **no contest**. This plea neither admits nor disputes a criminal charge, though it has the same effect as a guilty plea. It is often used as part of a plea bargain to reduce the severity of the criminal charges and the resulting punishment. This type of plea protects the defendant because the jury in a civil case will never hear about the criminal case. If the plaintiff later sues the defendant for the same thing in a civil case, the guilt in a criminal case cannot be used against him or her.

A fourth difference involves the burden of proof on the part of the plaintiff. In criminal cases the burden of proof must be beyond a reasonable doubt to render a guilty verdict, while in a civil case a preponderance of the evidence is all that is required to determine guilt. This essentially means that it was more likely than not that something happened in a certain way. The reason that these different standards exist is because civil liability is considered less blameworthy and the punishments are less severe than that of criminal liability.

The last difference I would like to point out between criminal and civil law involves appeals. In civil cases, an appeal can be made by either the plaintiff or the defendant, except in small claims actions where only the defendant can appeal. In criminal cases, only the defendant may appeal. However, the prosecution can appeal a number of legal questions, such as wrongful exclusion of evidence, but not the acquittal itself.

So far, we have covered Torts, Legal Research and Writing, Contracts, Civil Procedure, Criminal Law, as well as distinguishing between criminal and civil law. Let's take a moment to briefly go over what I encountered in my second semester Criminal Procedure class before moving onto a discussion of my Real Property class.

Criminal Procedure Constitutional Safeguards

Criminal procedure protects an individual's rights against the government. Specific constitutional safeguards are provided for those accused of crimes. These include:

1. The Fourth Amendment protection from unreasonable searches and seizure.
2. The requirement under the Fourth Amendment that a warrant for arrest cannot be issued without probable cause.
3. The requirement under the Fifth Amendment that no one can be deprived of life, liberty, or property without due process of law.

4. The prohibition under the Fifth Amendment against double jeopardy (trying someone twice for the same crime.)
5. The guarantees under the Sixth Amendment of a speedy trial, a trial by jury, a public trial, the right to confront a witness, and the right to an attorney at various stages of the criminal proceedings.
6. The prohibitions against excessive bails and fines as well as against cruel and unusual punishment.
7. The Fifth Amendment right against self-incrimination.

These are the major constitutional safeguards which serve to protect criminal defendants, and we spent an entire semester going over them in depth. And just like my other core classes, we learned about criminal procedure through briefing an endless array of cases. On an aside, the bar examination often has cross-overs in the essay portion of the exam. For example, criminal law issues are often crossed-over with issues of criminal procedure, so it's important to understand how everything relates to each other.

Sixth Amendment Right to Counsel

One of the cases we studied was *Gideon v. Wainwright*, 372 U.S. 335 (1963), which made the right of an indigent defendant in a criminal trial to the assistance of counsel applicable to the states by the Fourteenth Amendment. This case held that states are required to provide legal counsel to **indigent defendants** (those without sufficient income to afford a lawyer for defense in a criminal case).

Another case we studied which dealt with the right to counsel guaranteed by the Sixth Amendment was *Argersinger v. Hamlin*, 407 U.S. 25 (1972). In *Argersinger*, the defendant, an indigent, was convicted of carrying a concealed weapon, a misdemeanor punishable by up to six months in prison. The issue in the case was whether the Sixth Amendment right to assistance of counsel at trial extended to anyone accused of a crime that is punishable by imprisonment. The majority of the Supreme Court held that the answer to the issue is yes. In other words, the Sixth Amendment right to counsel at trial applies to anyone accused of a crime punishable by imprisonment. No accused may be deprived of his liberty as the result of any criminal prosecution, whether felony or misdemeanor, in which he was denied assistance of counsel.

Fourth Amendment Protection Against Unreasonable Searches and Seizures

We also spent a considerable amount of time in my Criminal Procedure class dealing with the concepts of arrest, search and seizure as defined within the scope of the Fourth Amendment. The Fourth Amendment, applicable to both the federal and state government, provides protection from unreasonable searches and seizures. Generally, evidence that is obtained by unreasonable search and seizure must be excluded.

Federal Exclusionary Rule

In the landmark case of *Mapp v. Ohio*, 367 U.S. 643 (1961), the United States Supreme Court ruled that evidence obtained in violation of the Fourth Amendment prohibition of unreasonable searches and seizures is inadmissible in state as well as federal courts. In addition, the Court held that the **federal exclusionary rule**, which forbids the use of unconstitutionally obtained evidence in federal courts, was also applicable to states. In other words, evidence obtained in violation of the Fourth Amendment cannot be used against someone in state or federal court.

The Fourth Amendment allows warrants based on probable cause, and in my Criminal Procedure class we studied *Chimel v. California*, 395 U.S. 752 (1969), which assessed the reasonableness of a search incident to an arrest. Police officers in this case had an arrest warrant for burglary, but not a search warrant. They served Chimel with the warrant and, despite his protests, they searched the entire home "on the basis of the lawful arrest." The search uncovered a number of items that were later used to convict him. The question on appeal was whether the warrantless search of Chimel's home was constitutionally justified under the Fourth Amendment as incident to the arrest. The Court held that the search was unreasonable under both the Fourth and Fourteenth Amendments, reasoning that searches "incident to arrest" are limited to the area within the immediate control of the suspect. Warrants and probable cause are important as they are necessary safeguards against government abuse.

A more current case that shows the evolution of the reasonableness of a search incident to arrest is *Riley v. California*, 573 U.S. _ (2014). In this landmark United States Supreme Court case, the Court unanimously held that the warrantless search and seizure of a cell phone during an arrest is unconstitutional. In other words, police generally need to obtain a warrant to search cell phones, even when it occurs during an otherwise lawful arrest.

The Court also emphasized that "the fact that technology now allows an individual to carry such information in his hand does not make the information any less worthy of the protection for which the Founders fought." As you can see from this brief discussion, despite modern technology, the courts still apply the applicable rules of law to determine whether a constitutional right has been violated. In *Riley*, a warrantless cell phone search was held to violate the Fourth Amendment right to privacy.

Essay Exam Writing Tips

I'd like at this point to share one of my Criminal Procedure essay exam questions that had to do with the Fourth Amendment prohibition against unreasonable searches and seizures, as well as how the individual states apply the exclusionary rule. We were given the following fact pattern and asked to discuss all the relevant issues.

Frank Hardy was arrested for possessing illegal drugs following a search of his automobile. The police had pulled him over for not having current license plate tags on his car and subsequently found drugs stashed in the glove compartment of his vehicle. They searched the car based on the fact that they smelled an odor in the car which resembled marijuana. The federal court convicted Frank for possessing marijuana based on the above search. Frank's attorneys are appealing the decision, claiming that the search was based on an illegal search and seizure. Now the state court wants to prosecute Frank as well.

At first glance, the above fact pattern seems pretty straight forward. However, there are many issues involved in this short fact pattern and the easiest way to tackle it is to make a short list of the issues and then discuss them individually. The first issue which popped into my head had to do with whether the state courts are required under the Fourteenth Amendment to follow the federal rule that evidence acquired through an unreasonable search and seizure is inadmissible. Another issue is whether the search of Frank's car was based on an illegal search and, if so, how the exclusionary rule applies. A third possible issue to discuss has to do with whether the search of Frank's glove compartment was a **protected** (any place where a person can reasonably expect privacy) or **unprotected** area. And finally, the issue becomes one of whether Frank's conviction can be overturned based upon an unreasonable search and seizure in violation of the Fourth Amendment.

Let's deal with the first issue using the **IRAC** approach which we discussed earlier in the Torts section of this diary. The **issue** is stated above, namely, whether the state courts are required to follow the federal rule that evidence acquired through an unreasonable search and seizure is inadmissible. The **rule of**

law is contained in *Mapp v. Ohio,* which states that all evidence obtained from illegal searches and seizures in violation of the Constitution is also inadmissible in state court. In the **analysis** and **conclusion,** I argued that if the federal court found that the search of Frank's car and the subsequent seizure of the marijuana was in violation of the Fourth Amendment, then the evidence also would be inadmissible in the state court based on the majority opinion of the *Mapp* case.

It is worth noting that while the U.S. Constitution sets the minimum level of protection for an individual's rights, states are free to provide even more protections to an individual's privacy rights. Depending on the state, they could pass laws placing greater restrictions on police when it comes to searching vehicles without a warrant.

The next issue would be whether the search of Frank's car was based on an illegal search, and, if so, how the exclusionary rule applies. The **rule of law** applicable to the above fact pattern is that the Fourth Amendment only prohibits *unreasonable* searches and seizures. A search warrant is required by police officers, but there are a few stated exceptions. Moveable vehicles may be searched on probable cause alone; there is no need for a warrant. Under the "automobile exception" to the search warrant requirement, courts have recognized that individuals have a lower expectation of privacy when driving a car than when they are in their homes.

In my **analysis,** I reasoned that there was probable cause to search Frank's vehicle for marijuana as the officers smelled the odor at the time of the routine traffic stop. In my **conclusion,** I stated that the police officers, in the course of a legitimate warrantless search of Frank's automobile, conducted a legal search and, hence, the exclusionary rule does not apply.

The next **issue** on this final exam hypothetical involved whether the search of Frank's glove compartment was a protected or non-protected area. As I stated above, the automobile exception allows the search of a lawfully stopped vehicle where there is probable cause. Based upon *United States v. Ross*, 456 U.S. 798 (1982), that search may include every part of the vehicle and its contents that may conceal the object of the search.

In my **analysis,** I maintained that Frank could not reasonably expect privacy as to the contents of his car glove compartment, especially in light of the Supreme Court's ruling in *United States v. Ross*. The Court in that case held that "police officers who have legitimately stopped an automobile and who have probable cause to believe that contraband is concealed somewhere within it may conduct a warrantless search of the vehicle that is as thorough as a magistrate could authorize by warrant." In **conclusion,** I maintained that Frank's glove compartment was not a protected area evoking Fourth Amendment protection.

The last **issue** I talked about on this Criminal Procedure exam essay was whether Frank's conviction could be overturned based upon an unreasonable search and seizure claim in violation of the Fourth Amendment. Generally, evidence that is obtained by unreasonable search and seizure must be excluded. However, in this hypothetical, I reasoned that the search of Frank's car and the subsequent seizure of marijuana was conducted based on a lawful search pursuant to probable cause. In general, **probable**

cause refers to the requirement that police have adequate reason to arrest someone, conduct a search, or seize property. The reason automobiles may be searched on probable cause alone has to do with a car's mobility, as well as a diminished expectation of privacy. In **conclusion**, I contended that Frank's conviction should not be overturned based upon an unreasonable search and seizure.

On your final essay exams in law school, and also in the practice of the law itself, what counts is *how* you come to your final conclusion, using the IRAC approach. I realized that my professors have a checklist of issues they want the students to spot. As long as you discuss the relevant issues, state the applicable law, and then use legal analysis to form your conclusion, you are well on your way to writing a top-notch final exam essay. There are a lot of gray areas in the law, and your law professor is much more interested in how you apply to the rule of law to the issues on the exam, as opposed to having the right or wrong answer. It is in the analysis that differentiates from an A or B grade.

Furthermore, you need not cite specific cases on your final exam to do well. I only included them in my analysis above to show you how to incorporate key cases in your final exam essays if you want to. Many times, first year law students are so nervous during their final exams that they freeze up and forget the names of certain landmark cases they had studied. That actually happened to me on my Civil Procedure final essay exam. Don't worry about that aspect. As I said earlier, if you can remember cases well known for their rule of law (or an important dissenting opinion), try to incorporate them into your writing; however, if you can't remember cases to include, the professor will not penalize you for it so long as you can clearly identify the issues and rules of law contained in the particular fact pattern you are given.

Here are 4 steps I recommend for taking written exams:

1. Notice how much time you have for the problem. Time is your enemy on law school exams (most exams are one hour)
2. Go to the end of the problem you are given and find the question first. Then go back and scan the facts
3. Now go back and read the problem more carefully
4. Re-read the fact pattern and identify the issues, as you pick out facts to support the issues

Ideally you should allot thirty to forty minutes to plan your essay and twenty minutes to write or type your answer. Use the IRAC approach for each issue you spot. If you spot all the issues and rules, you are most likely to receive a B grade on the exam. If you miss an issue or state an incorrect rule of law, you are likely to receive a C grade. Thus, it is vital that you know the rules of law for your written exams. Getting to a top A grade is in your analysis. Your conclusion really doesn't matter so long as it is supported by your analysis.

As you can see from the above final examination essay question for my Criminal Procedure class, it is important to be well-organized during your first year of law school so that you can immediately spot the issues and apply the applicable rule of law to a particular fact pattern. In fact, the key to a successful first year is organization. You need to gather the facts, find the relevant law, and then combine the law and the facts into a pattern that tells a story. This approach is used for many audiences, which include your law professors, the bar examiners, and finally the practice of law itself, in which your main audience is your client and the judge or jury before whom you are arguing his or her case.

Taking law school exams is a skill and preparing for exams is different than preparing for class. For instance, classroom daily preparation includes briefing cases, outlining, and distilling applicable rules of law. Preparing for exams deals with going over IRAC by getting old exams and practicing this method on them. Many law schools have copies of past law school examinations on file with the library, and you can search for exams either by class name or by professor.

I was beginning to get the hang of things now that I had attended five of the six classes of my first semester schedule. The last class was Real Property, which was scheduled for 2:30 p.m. that afternoon, so I had time for a long lunch. I actually breathed a sigh of relief as I made my way to the now familiar classroom C.

CHAPTER 9

Real Property Law

In this chapter...

- ✓ Real property v. personal property
- ✓ Adverse possession
- ✓ Easements
- ✓ Possessory estates
- ✓ Future interests

REAL PROPERTY ROUNDED out my first semester legal studies as we previously had dealt with tortious behavior, contracts, criminal behavior, the civil procedure process, and legal research and writing.

Real Property v. Personal Property

Real property (also known as **real estate** or **immoveable property**) law has to do with land ownership or possession. It includes not only the soil, natural products (such as timber and water) and artificial structures and fixtures on the earth's surface, but also the waters and minerals under the surface and the air space above it. Contrast **personal property**, which refers to **movable items** and, essentially, all owned items that are *not* real property.

The **legal definition of personal property** is "anything besides land that may be subject to ownership." In other words, personal property is something that you can pick up or move around. There are two basic types of personal property: **tangible** and **intangible**. Tangible refers to physical property that can be physically touched such as cars, books, jewelry, bank accounts, money, etc. Intangible property is non-physical property such as patents, trademarks, copyrights, debts, company goodwill, and trade secrets. In my first year Real Property class we learned about the different ways to acquire both personal as well as real property, and the ownership rights involved in both of these types of property.

Like so much of our law in the United States, the laws governing the purchase, possession, and sale of property date back to the **English common law,** which is basically the legal system developed in England in the 11th century and which is still being followed today. What makes English law unique is that it is based on applying legal precedent (*stare decisis*) to present and future decisions made by judges. This is important as judges are obliged to make their rulings as consistent as reasonably possible with the previous judicial decisions on the same subject.

Adverse Possession

We spent a great deal of time on the concept of **adverse possession** during the first few weeks of class. I had no idea what adverse possession was, but the concept is relatively simple. It is defined as a method of acquiring legal title to land through actual, continuous and open occupancy of the property for a prescribed period of time, under claim of right, and in opposition to the rights of the true owner.

In other words, property may be occupied by one who does not own the property. The doctrine of adverse possession creates an obligation on the part of the title holder of property to eject, within a state statutorily prescribed period, a wrongful possessor of the land. Provided that certain other elements are met, a titleholder who fails this obligation will lose his or her title to the land in question to the adverse possessor.

The woman sitting to my right was asked by our professor to tell the class the facts of the *Van Valkenburgh v. Lutz*, 304 N.Y. 95, 106 N.E.2d 28 (1952), case. She stated nervously that this case involved an appeal by Van Valkenburgh, the appellant, from the lower court's decision which granted title to Lutz, the appellee, under a claim of title of adverse possession. For several years, the Lutzes had traveled over neighboring land they did not own. A few years later, the Valkenburghs purchased the land that the Lutzes traveled over and built a fence across the area that the Lutzes claimed a right to use. Lutz filed a lawsuit in lower court (he was the plaintiff) against Valkenburgh (the defendant) claiming his right of way was being interfered with. The trial court found in favor of Lutz and Valkenburgh appealed.

Satisfied with the response, the professor then asked me what I thought the issue was in the case. I was dumbfounded that I could be called upon so much in only two days of school. Since I had briefed the case the night before at midnight, I dutifully answered that the issue was a question as to what facts are necessary to satisfy the **actual**, **hostile**, and **under claim of right** requirements of acquiring title by adverse possession. In other words, was title acquired to the land in question by virtue of adverse possession? I knew the court's holding and rule of law in the case, and was prepared to answer when the professor called upon yet another fellow student. However, instead of asking for those elements of the brief, he shocked us all by asking what the other elements were for acquiring title by adverse possession. This made us all stop and think because the answer was not found in the *Van Valkenburgh* case at all. The **continuous use** requirement was found in the *Howard v. Kunto*, 3 Wn. App. 393, 477 P.2d 210 (Ct. App. 1970), case. The other two requirements involved proving that the occupancy is **exclusive**, as well as **open and notorious**.

I mention this because it showed us that professors all have different styles of testing the student's knowledge of the material covered in the textbook. Our property professor was trying to get our minds off the mundane drudgery of briefing cases to see the broader picture and also to keep us off balance. In essence, you need to be adequately prepared for all your classes during your first year of law school because you will never know what will happen in class.

Getting back to the *Van Valkenburgh* case, the professor gave us a break and explained to us the rule of law concerning the requirement of actual possession. It is satisfied when the adverse possessor improves, cultivates, or encloses the premises to such an extent that he generally *appears* to be the rightful owner.

The **hostile** and under claim of right requirement is met if the adverse possessor knows that he is not the rightful owner of the property but claims it as his own anyway. In this context, **hostile** does not mean "unfriendly"; instead it means that the possession infringes on the rights of the true owner. One cannot succeed in claiming adverse possession if it is kept secret. The public policy behind adverse possession is to encourage owners to remover trespassers in a timely manner. Basically, adverse possession is the transfer of an interest in land without the consent of the prior owner and even in spite of the dissent of the owner. This type of forced conveyance provides for the efficient allocation of scarce resources, protects third party purchasers, and allows the adverse possessor to move on with his or her life.

I particularly enjoyed our study of adverse possession, sometimes described as **"squatter's rights"**, because during my first semester of law school I was able to help out a friend who was dealing with such a problem. The study of law really seems worth it when you can apply what you have learned to a real-life situation.

My friend's neighbor built a garage which overlapped a considerable amount over my friend's land. For over five years, my friend never said anything to his neighbor about the garage, which extended three feet over his property. One day, they got into a heated dispute as my friend's neighbor claimed that he owned the property where the garage encroached on my friend's land through adverse possession.

From my knowledge of adverse possession from my property class, I told my friend that California adverse possession laws require at least five years of possession *and* payment of property taxes throughout the period in order to be able to eligible for legal title. Thus, I suggested that my friend first find out whether his neighbor had paid the property taxes; if so, he might have a claim for adverse possession if all the other elements are met. Namely, if his neighbor had continuously used the property with my friend's knowledge for the five-year period, and had paid the property taxes, he might have a claim. But if the taxes were not paid, then he would not be able to claim the property through the legal doctrine of adverse possession.

Many landowners, like my neighbor, can be surprised to learn that under certain circumstances a trespasser can come onto their land, occupy it, and gain legal ownership of it, whether it be a few feet of property or whole acres. Landowners should be alert to the risk of someone using their property, even a small strip on the edge.

A trespasser may also gain a legal right to use a part of someone else's property through a **prescriptive easement.** A prescriptive easement is generally created when someone uses land for access, such as a driveway, beach path, or shortcut; however, it can also occur when a neighbor begins to use part of an adjoining property. After the time period requirement is met, the trespasser gains a legal right to *use* the property but does not get ownership rights like with adverse possession.

Going back to my friend's problem, where his neighbor built a garage partly on his land, a court could give his neighbor a prescriptive easement allowing him to use the three feet of garage on my friend's property. The building of a garage could be seen as substantial enough to create a prescriptive easement; however, my friend's neighbor would not own the land, but rather have the legal right to use it.

There was also another option for my friend. He could have simply granted his neighbor the permission to use the property, effectively canceling his claim to a prescriptive easement. A *prescriptive easement* is an *easement* that is earned by regular use; it is not something that is purchased, negotiated, or granted. Giving permission to a current user also prevents neighbors who move in later from claiming they have inherited a prescriptive easement. My friend actually had a talk with his neighbor based on our discussion and decided to give his neighbor permission to use his property for the overlapping garage, thus negating any adverse claims to the property.

Easements

From the above discussion, you can see how an **easement** is basically a right to cross or otherwise use someone else's land for a specified purpose. There are two types of easements which grant a nonpossessory property interest to the easement holder, giving that person permission to use another's land. Contrast this to adverse possession, where there is no permission to use the land.

The first type of easement is an **affirmative easement**, which gives the easement holder the right to do something on the grantor of the easement's land. An example of this type of easement is for a landowner to allow another person to travel on the road through his or her land. A **negative easement**, on the other hand, allows the easement holder to prevent the person granting the easement from doing something lawful on his or her own land. An example of this would be to allow someone to build a structure on his or her property that obscures light or a scenic view of a neighbor.

Easements can be created by **express grant**, by **implication**, by **necessity**, and by **adverse possession**. Easements can also be terminated in three ways:

1. If the easement was created by necessity and the necessity ceases to exist;
2. If the land is destroyed; or
3. If the easement was abandoned.

The rest of the year we focused on the following subjects dealing with real property law: possessory estates, future interests, co-ownership and marital interests, landlord-tenant law, the land transaction, title assurance, private land-use arrangements, nuisance zoning, and **eminent domain** (eminent domain is defined as the right of the government or its agent to take private property for public use with the payment of compensation). Again, we learned the rules governing these various areas of real estate law through studying the cases in our textbook.

Possessory Estates

I'd like to briefly give you an overview of **possessory estates**. An estate is basically an interest in land that is or may become possessory and is measured by some period of time. The types of possessory estates we studied were:

1. **Fee simple** estates have the potential of lasting forever, such as absolute ownership;
2. **Fee tail** estates also have the potential to last forever, but will cease if and when the first fee tail tenant has no lineal descendants to succeed him or her in possession of the estate;
3. **Life estates** end upon the death of a person; and
4. **Leasehold estates** last for any fixed calendar period (**term of years**), or from period to period until the landlord or tenant gives notice to terminate (**periodic tenancy**), or so long as both the landlord and tenant desire (**tenancy at will**).

In landlord-tenant law, we learned about leaseholds, the obligations of both the landlord and tenant, landlord's remedies, and assignment and subleasing. The difference between a **leasehold** and a **freehold** is that in the former you have a landlord, and in the latter, you own the property outright.

Future Interests

Future interests, on the other hand, are non-possessory interests that can become possessory in the future. In other words, the interest does not include a current right of ownership and a landowner with a future interest does not have any present rights or privileges as far as the land is concerned. We also studied the common law **rule against perpetuities,** which basically states that certain interests in property must vest, if at all, within twenty-one years after the death of a life in being at the time the interest was created. In other words, this rule is a way to prevent a person from drafting a transfer agreement that could control the future of the land he or she is giving up fifty to hundreds of years after he or she is gone. It prevents people from using a deed or will to control the ownership of property for an extended period of time past the lives of people living at the time the deed or will was written.

Hopefully you can see that the study and preparation process is the same for every core subject. You will be asked to read a long list of cases from your textbook and then distill the relevant legal principles using your case briefs. Let's now move onto a short discussion of Evidence, which, although often taught during your second year of law school, is still worthy of a cursory analysis as this course is tested on the bar examination.

CHAPTER 10

Evidence

In this chapter...

✓ Difference between criminal law, criminal procedure, and evidence
✓ Burden of proof
✓ The Brady Rule
✓ Types of evidence
✓ Hearsay
✓ Presumptions
✓ Other rules of evidence

AS WE DISCUSSED in the introduction to this book, the Multistate Bar Examination (MBE) covers seven legal practice areas: Torts, Contracts, Civil Procedure, Criminal Law and Procedure, Real Property, Evidence, and Constitutional Law. We have already talked about my personal experiences in my Torts, Contracts, Civil Procedure, Criminal Law and Procedure, and Real Property classes. This chapter will introduce you to the **law of evidence**, also known as the **rules of evidence**. This course is recommended by many law schools for students who plan to take trial advocacy classes or other clinical offerings.

Differences between Criminal Law, Criminal Procedure, and Evidence

You may be wondering what the differences are between Criminal Law, Criminal Procedure, and Evidence, so let me briefly explain here. In **Criminal Law**, the focus is on whether a crime was committed, what type of crime, and what the defenses are to that crime. **Criminal Procedure** deals with the legal processes and responsibilities the government must adhere to when investigating, questioning and prosecuting an accused individual. **Evidence**, on the other hand, encompasses the rules and legal principles that govern the presentation of the facts of a legal proceeding. In simple terms, the dictionary definition of evidence is "the information that is used in a court of law to try to prove something. Evidence is obtained from documents, objects, or witnesses."

I took Evidence in the spring semester of my second year of law school, which is typical as this course is generally not part of the first year curriculum. However, I chose to include a *brief* discussion of Evidence in this diary, as it is not only tested on the MBE, but also covers important rules that attorneys use to find proof that best supports their client's case. The **Federal Rules of Evidence** govern the admissibility of evidence in federal trials, and state rules of evidence are largely modeled after the federal rules.

Burden of Proof

On a practical level, an attorney may challenge and/or try to suppress evidence presented by the other party in both criminal and civil trials. One of the main differences between the use of evidence in criminal and civil cases is the *burden of proof*. In a criminal trial, the prosecution must prove guilt "beyond a reasonable doubt," while for a civil defendant to be found liable, the plaintiff generally need only prove culpability "by a preponderance of the evidence," which requires a lower threshold of proof.

My professor for this class was a judge and an adjunct professor. **Adjunct professors** teach on a limited-term contract, often for one semester at a time, and are ineligible for tenure. The first day of class he told us that in addition to studying **American federal law** (the Federal Rules of Evidence and cases interpreting them), we would also study some state rules and cases. I realized that the study of case law was not going away! However, I definitely felt better prepared to read and analyze the massive amounts of cases in our textbook due to having a year of law school under my belt.

The Brady Rule

One landmark case we studied was *Brady v. Maryland*, 373 U.S. 83 (1963), which established the **Brady Rule**. The United States Supreme Court held that the prosecution must turn over all

exculpatory evidence (evidence tending to clear one from a charge of fault or guilt) that might acquit the defendant. Thus, according to the Brady Rule, the prosecution must disclose known evidence or information favorable to the defendant in a criminal case.

Types of Evidence

We learned that evidence is crucial in both civil and criminal proceedings, and may include blood or hair samples, video surveillance recordings or witness testimony. Further, we studied the four general types of evidence.

1. **Real evidence** (tangible things, such as a weapon);
2. **Demonstrative** (a model of what likely happened at a given time and place);
3. **Documentary** (a letter, blog post, or other document); and
4. **Testimonial** (witness testimony).

Circumstantial evidence refers to evidence that does not come from direct observation of a fact in issue, such as fingerprints at the scene of the crime. It is often called **indirect evidence**, which is distinguished from **direct evidence**, which supports the truth of a claim directly without inference. An example of direct evidence is an eyewitness actually seeing the defendant shoot the victim.

Corroborating evidence is evidence that strengthens, adds to, authenticates, or confirms already existing evidence. It is independent and different from evidence already presented as proof of a factual matter. An example would be where a witness saw the accused leaving the crime scene (**direct evidence**), accompanied by physical evidence, such as fingerprints, which place the defendant at the crime scene.

Hearsay

Hearsay is a statement made out of court which is offered as proof of the truth of the matter asserted. It is generally inadmissible under Federal Rule of Evidence 801(c). We learned some hearsay exemptions under *Fed. R. Evid. 84*, which I will talk about in my Evidence outline in the third part of this book. The goal of the hearsay rule is to make sure the evidence at trial is as reliable as possible. For example, if Tom is on trial for murder, Barry cannot testify that he heard Anne say that before the events in question Tom had a gun and was acting out of control. The court needs Anne's testimony regarding her exact observations, not Barry's secondhand story about what Anne allegedly saw happen.

Presumptions

We also studied **presumptions,** which are conclusions that the **trier of fact** (the judge in a bench trial or jury in a jury trial that carries the responsibility of determining the issues of fact in a case) is required to draw from the evidence, and we went over the two burdens of proof in evidence: **burden of production** (providing evidence to show that facts exist) and **burden of persuasion** (presenting legally sufficient evidence to persuade the trier of fact on all issues.) For those of you who do not know, a **bench trial** is a trial by judge as opposed to a trial by jury.

Other Rules of Evidence

Other areas of evidence which we studied in depth were **judicial notice** (the acceptance of a fact as true without the necessity of formal proof; e.g. public and court records, tides, times of sunset and sunrise); **relevance** (pertains to whether the evidence tends to prove or disprove a fact of consequence); **privileges** (the state and common law principles based on societal desires to encourage particular relationships such as spousal communications, attorney-client communications, psychotherapist-client and social worker-client privileges); **examination and impeachment of witnesses;** and the *best evidence rule,* which is a legal principle that holds an original copy of a document as superior authentication.

Another important legal rule you will encounter in your Evidence class is the **exclusionary rule**. It excludes evidence obtained in violation of a defendant's constitutional rights. This is an example of a crossover between the classes of Evidence and Criminal Procedure. Remember how we talked about the decision in *Mapp v. Ohio*, 367 U.S. 643 (1961) in our discussion of my Criminal Procedure class? The court's decision in that case established that the exclusionary rule applies to evidence gained from an unreasonable search or seizure in violation of the Fourth Amendment. This rule prevents the government from using most evidence gathered in violation of the United States Constitution, referring to the rights of the Fourth Amendment that protects against unreasonable searches as well as the Due Process Clause of the Fourteenth Amendment.

Due process means that every person is entitled to certain safeguards that help ensure that a trial is fair and impartial. Some basic due process rights include the right to be assisted by a lawyer, the right to a neutral decision maker (jury or judge), the right to know the charges against you, the right to question witnesses against you, and the right to present testimony in your favor.

This is a good lead-in for the final core subject in this diary, namely Constitutional Law, in which we studied the rights carved out by the federal and state constitutions.

CHAPTER 11

Constitutional Law

In this chapter...

- ✓ The United States Constitution
- ✓ Judicial review
- ✓ Original and appellate jurisdiction
- ✓ Certiorari
- ✓ Justiciability
- ✓ Standing
- ✓ Ripeness
- ✓ Other constitutional law concepts
- ✓ Exam formats

LET'S MOVE NOW to the last core subject covered in one's first year of law school and also on the bar examination, namely, Constitutional Law. As I noted earlier, I did not take this course until my second year of law school; nonetheless it is a fundamental course and worthy of discussion. Many law schools teach Constitutional Law (also referred to as "Con Law") in the first year and others may wait and teach it during the second or third year; it varies from school to school. This course is as close to a history class as you will take during your first year, with its emphasis on issues of government structure and individual rights.

Black's Law Dictionary defines Constitutional Law as follows:

"That branch of the public law of a nation or state which treats of the organization, powers and frame of government, the distribution of political and governmental authorities and functions, the fundamental principles which are to regulate the relations of government and citizen, and which prescribes generally the plans and method according to which the public affairs of the nation or state are to be administered."

Henry Campbell Black
Black's Law Dictionary
(Saint Paul, Minn.: West Publishing
Co., 1983)

The United States Constitution

The United States Constitution is the supreme law of the land and is often called **super law**, as any laws which violate the Constitution are void. Similarly, each individual state constitution is **supreme** within the state, so long as it does not conflict with the United States Constitution.

Thus, a constitution is simply the fundamental principles of law by which a government is created and a country (or state) administered. Constitutional law can be distinguished from statutory law in that the latter is the rules, or statutes, decided by legislative representatives, and statutes are subject to the limitations of the Constitution. Further, **constitutional rights** are the individual liberties granted by state and federal constitutions which protect citizens from government interference. We previously touched upon several constitutional rights afforded to criminal defendants in our discussion of criminal procedure.

The United States Constitution defines the powers and limitations of the federal government. **Article I** defines the power to make laws by the legislature; **Article II** defines how those laws are to be carried out through the executive branch of the government; and **Article III** defines the laws through the judicial branch of the government.

We began our study of constitutional law by studying the nature and source of the Supreme Court's authority to review congressional acts, state laws, and state court judgments. Next, we focused on Congress' authority to limit federal court jurisdiction. As you can see, the study of jurisdiction not only applies to civil procedure, but to constitutional law as well. To refresh your memory, jurisdiction is basically the authority of a court to hear a case.

Just like in all my other classes, the professor asked us about the assigned material to test our ability to cipher through the cases and find the relevant law. The difference was that I was taking this course in my second year of law school, where students are generally not called out individually but instead raise their hands to participate in answering questions.

Judicial Review

One of the first cases we studied was *Marbury v. Madison*, 5 U.S. 137 (1803), which established the doctrine of **judicial review**. This is the power of the federal courts to declare legislative acts unconstitutional and thus void. The unanimous opinion of the court was written by Chief Justice John Marshall.

In this landmark case, William Marbury had been appointed as a justice of the peace for the District of Columbia in the final hours of the Adams administration. When James Madison, Thomas Jefferson's new secretary of state, refused to deliver Marbury's commission, Marbury, joined by three other similarly situated appointees, petitioned for a writ of mandamus compelling delivery of the commission. A **writ of mandamus** is a command by a superior court to a public official or lower court to perform a special duty. There were three issues that the court addressed in *Marbury*:

1. Whether Marbury had a right to receive his commission;
2. Whether he could sue for his commission in court; and
3. Whether the Supreme Court has the authority to order the delivery of his commission.

Marbury argued that the Judiciary Act of 1789 gave the Supreme Court original jurisdiction over his case. This act authorized the Supreme Court to issue writs of mandamus to persons holding office under the authority of the United States. The court held that, although Marbury had a right to receive his commission and that a writ of mandamus was the proper way to seek a remedy, he could not sue for it in court.

Chief Justice Marshall stated that the provision of the Judiciary Act of 1789, enabling Marbury to bring his claim to the Supreme Court was unconstitutional, as it extended the Court's original jurisdiction beyond that which Article III, Section 2, established. The Supreme Court stated in *Marbury* that Article III, Section 2, Clause 2, of the Constitution authorizes original jurisdiction only in cases involving "Ambassadors, other public Ministers and Consuls, and those in which a State shall be Party."

Since the dispute between Marbury and Madison did not involve ambassadors, public ministers, consuls, or states, Chief Justice Marshall held that the Supreme Court did not have the authority to exercise its original jurisdiction. He further held that Congress did not have the power to modify the Constitution through regular legislation because the Supremacy Clause places the Constitution before the laws. According to the Court, the Constitution gives the judicial branch the power to strike down laws passed by Congress, the legislative branch.

Thus, Marshall, through the holding in *Marbury*, established the principle of judicial review, where the actions of the legislative branch of government are subject to review and possible invalidation by the judiciary. If you can understand the gist of this complicated case, you will be well ahead of the game when you encounter it in law school.

Original and Appellate Jurisdiction

We also learned about original jurisdiction from studying *Marbury v. Madison*. Basically, jurisdiction of the courts in the United States is divided into two categories, **original** and **appellate jurisdiction**. The authority of a court to decide a case based upon trial and evidence rather than on the basis of appeal is called original jurisdiction, while appellate jurisdiction refers to the authority of a court to hear a case upon appeal from a lower court.

The Supreme Court has original jurisdiction over cases of interpretation of the Constitution and whether the dispute is between states and between the federal government and a state. Very few cases come to the Supreme Court under original jurisdiction; the majority of the cases heard by the Supreme Court pertain to those falling under appellate jurisdiction.

The Supreme Court's authority to review the constitutionality of state laws is stated in Article VI, Clause 2 (**the Supremacy Clause**), as well as in Article III, Section 2, of the United States Constitution:

> "Article III, Section 2. The judicial Power shall extend to all Cases, in Law and Equity, arising under this Constitution, the Laws of the United States, and Treaties made, or which shall be made, under their Authority;—to all Cases affecting Ambassadors, other public ministers and Consuls;—to all Cases of admiralty and maritime Jurisdiction;—to Controversies to which the

United States shall be a Party;—**to Controversies between two or more States;— between a State and Citizens of another State;—between Citizens of different States;—between Citizens of the same State claiming Lands under Grants of different States, and between a State, or the Citizens thereof**, and foreign States, Citizens or Subjects."

Further, the Supreme Court can only review a state court's decision under the Court's appellate jurisdiction. In this context, appellate jurisdiction refers to the power vested in the United States Supreme Court to correct legal errors of state courts and to revise their judgments accordingly. Review of state court judgments is limited to federal questions decided in state courts.

Thus, the Constitution gives the Supreme Court its original jurisdiction or power to hear and determine a case. Congress may not add or take away from that jurisdiction; however, the Supreme Court in *Ex Parte McCardle*, 74 U.S. 506 (1869), held that the Supreme Court exercises its appellate jurisdiction at Congress' discretion.

Certiorari

Prior to 1988 there were two ways for a case to be heard by the Supreme Court, either by **appeal** or by **certiorari**. Before 1988, the Court was compelled to hear all cases that came before it on appeal. In 1988, however, Congress all but eliminated the mandatory appeal process. Today nearly every case heard by the United

States Supreme Court gets there by the process of certiorari.

Simply stated, certiorari is the process by which the Supreme Court determines which cases it will hear. Due to the fact that the court has total discretion in granting or denying certiorari, it now has full control of the nature and number of cases it hears.

In order to be eligible for certiorari, a case must be based on federal law and four of the nine Justices must cast votes approving such a grant (known as the four vote requirement.) In other words, **four** of the **nine Justices** must vote to accept a case. If the above two elements are met, the Court will grant certiorari in any of the following instances:

1. Conflicts between different federal courts of appeal;
2. Conflicts between the highest courts of two states;
3. Conflict between a state's highest court and a federal court of appeals; and
4. A state court or federal court of appeals decision involving an important question not yet settled by the Supreme Court.

Of course, the above information was not as simply stated in our textbook as I laid it out for you. Rather, we garnered the pertinent facts regarding the authority of the Supreme Court from the cases in our textbook (just like all the other core classes I have previously covered).

Justiciability

Furthermore, we learned that the Supreme Court and lower federal courts will only hear **justiciable** cases. Justiciability refers to the types of matters that the federal courts can adjudicate. If a case is *nonjusticiable,* a federal court cannot hear it.

To be justiciable, five things must occur:

1. The court must not be offering an advisory opinion;
2. The plaintiff must have standing;
3. The issues must be ripe;
4. The issues cannot be moot; and
5. The issues cannot violate the political question doctrine.

Let's look briefly at these elements of the authority of the federal court to assert jurisdiction through justiciable cases. Federal courts will not issue advisory opinions, which are issued in the absence of a case or controversy. This rule is based on the constitutional guarantee of separation of powers in Article III of the United States Constitution. Federal courts only have constitutional authority to resolve actual disputes.

Standing

A plaintiff must have **standing** for a case to be justiciable. Standing is basically the legal right to initiate a lawsuit. We studied *Allen v. Wright,* 468 U.S. 737 (1984), where the court stated that "in essence the question of standing is whether the litigant is entitled to have the court decide the merits of the dispute or of particular issues." Since I was in law school, the Supreme Court has developed a three-part test for Article III standing as found in *Lujan v. Defenders of Wildlife,* 504 U.S. 555 (1992):

1. There must be an injury in fact (an invasion of a legally protected interest);
2. There must be a causal relationship between the injury and the challenged conduct; and
3. There must be a likelihood that the injury will be redressed by a favorable decision.

Ripeness

The next requirement for a case to be justiciable is **ripeness**. A claim is *"ripe"* when the facts of the case have matured into an existing, substantial controversy warranting judicial intervention. Further, a case cannot be **moot**. Mootness occurs when there is no longer an actual controversy between the parties to a court case. Thus, there would be no actual impact by a court ruling. A U.S. federal court must dismiss a case if the issues in it have become moot. Parties must be involved in an actual dispute for a federal case to be justiciable; the court cannot take on a purely hypothetical debate where there is no potential relief that the court can grant.

Lastly, for a case to be justiciable it cannot violate the **political question doctrine**; a court will not adjudicate a question that would be better resolved by the other branches of government due to its inherently political nature.

Other Constitutional Law Concepts

We also spent a great deal of time discussing cases involving the **Bill of Rights**, as many constitutional issues involve these first ten amendments to the U.S. Constitution. These amendments contain such rights as the freedom of speech, the right to a fair trial, and the right to be free from certain types of discrimination. Then, for the rest of the semester we studied the concepts of national power and commerce power, state regulation and the national economy, separation of powers, procedural due process, substantive due process, equal protection, post-Civil War amendments and civil rights legislation, freedom of expression, and finally the Constitution and religion.

Exam Formats

Now's a good time to discuss the format for my exams for most of my first year core classes. It varied from class to class, but generally our midterms were essay format, while our final exam consisted of essays and multiple-choice questions. The essays were usually a hypothetical fact pattern with a client, and the multiple choice were based on the IRAC approach. In terms of my Legal Research and Writing Class, the midterm was multiple choice format and the answers were based on comprehension and recall, rather than IRAC. In this class, we also were graded on the various papers that we wrote throughout the year.

This discussion is what I experienced at Pepperdine Law School; other law schools may have different exam formats. At the beginning of the semester your professors will give you an overview of not only the format of the midterms and exams, but also the percentage of your grade that each component will be worth. For me, the key to writing an organized law school essay was to:

1. Outline my answers first;
2. Use lots of subheadings; and
3. Write legibly.

PEPPERDINE UNIVERSITY

SCHOOL OF LAW

EXAM BOOK

STUDENT NUMBER 3052   DATE 4-28-87

COURSE Constit Law   SECTION

PROFESSOR

Q1 = 95
Q2 = 24 = 88
MC 20-86

90+1 91

BOOK NUMBER ① FOR QUESTION NUMBER

TOTAL BOOKS FOR THIS EXAM

Table 11.1

Some law schools allow you to use computers to write the essays, but the traditional format is to write your answers in a blue composition book, which is different than the other dreaded *Bluebook*, which deals with the proper legal citations. Table 11.1 shows my actual graded exam blue book from Constitutional Law.

As I mentioned earlier, Constitutional Law proved to be one of my *fortes*, as I received an American Jurisprudence award for the course. This award is given to the student with the highest grade in a particular class. I was thrilled to finally discover that my previous academic record could indeed translate itself into law school. It just took some time for me to adapt to the different style of law school.

My exam was divided up into three sections: two essay questions and one multiple choice section. The first question dealt with issues regarding freedom of expression, freedom of religion, as well as substantive due process.

The second question dealt with issues of state action, the equal protection component of the due process clause of the Fifth Amendment, and the First Amendment regulation of obscenity. I mention the issues that were contained in the fact patterns of my two Constitutional Law essays because it shows how a professor can focus in on certain areas of the law covered and not others.

There were many areas of Constitutional Law which were not covered on that written portion of our final. Many of these areas were contained in questions in the multiple choice section.

However, in some classes the exams are solely essays, with no multiple choice. Each professor has a different approach. It is difficult, if not impossible, for a professor to write a factual scenario which encompasses all the concepts covered during the course of a semester, so he or she will pick and choose which ones to focus on in the exam. It is of utmost importance that you study *all* of the material covered during a semester of a particular course, because you never know what particular area might be emphasized on the final.

Let's go back to my Legal Research and Writing class and explore the technique for writing legal papers in the next chapter.

CHAPTER 12

Legal Research and Writing Revisited

In this chapter...

✓ The office memorandum
✓ Key elements of an office memorandum
✓ The legal brief

NOW THAT I have covered all of the basic subjects which I encountered during my first year of law school, I would like to go back to the subject of Legal Research and Writing before wrapping up this part of my diary. Hopefully you can now see how this subject is interrelated to all of your other core classes.

During the course of the class, we learned how to find, understand, and apply the law, and then communicate that analysis clearly and effectively. We were also assigned blue book exercises to comprehend the essential rules for legal practitioners found in *The Bluebook*. Our teacher told us that citation skills can only be acquired through practice. We did a series of exercises, organized by topic, which progressed from basic citation forms to more advanced citation rules, all designed to help us master legal citation through these interactive exercises.

Remember our discussion earlier about how *The Bluebook* is the unique system of citation law students, lawyers, scholars, judges, and other legal professionals rely on in their writing? To make things even more complex, these Legal Research and Writing blue book exercises are not to be confused with that other blue book in which you will write your law school exam essays.

We also studied in depth two aspects of legal writing, namely the **office memorandum** and the **brief**, which are two of the most widely used documents by attorneys in the course of their daily work.

Law Office Memorandum

The office memorandum is a basic document of legal writing, as legal advice to a client is often based on a formal memorandum of law. This memo is written to predict what effect the application of the relevant law will have on the client's situation. Senior attorneys use memorandums to determine what advice to give a client. One of our major projects in our Legal Research and Writing class was to write an office memorandum.

There are two types of memos we covered: open and closed. An **open memorandum** was an assignment in which we were asked to find the **primary authorities** for that memo ourselves versus a **closed memo** in which we could only use the authorities provided to us. A primary authority is a term used in legal research which refers to statements of law that are binding upon the courts, governments and individuals. Here is an example of a closed memorandum we were assigned:

MEMORANDUM
Date: September 7, 1987
To: Legal Research & Writing Section 1
Re: Closed Memo Discussion Section and Full Memo
Your first major assignment is a memo discussion section and a full memo. Both revolve around the set of facts below. Using these facts and the law that I'll provide, you will create arguments for both parties. Try to organize the story in your head as you read over the facts. The discussion section addresses two issues, and you need to explain the law that governs the first issue, describe the argument for both parties as they relate to that issue, and then make a prediction about which party will likely prevail on that issue. Then you need to repeat the process for the second issue. Later, for the full memo you will add all the other parts of the office memo that I will describe to you later this semester.

Table 12.1

For the sake of brevity, and not to completely overwhelm you, I am eliminating the two page fact summary which was part of this assignment. The real take-away for you is to see the type of assignment you will be doing, not only in your Legal Research and Writing class, but also in the practice of law itself. Each law school will teach this information a bit differently, as each professor has a distinct style. However, the basics will be the essentially the same.

Key Elements of an Office Memorandum

Let's move on to a discussion of the format I learned at Pepperdine as to how to write an office memorandum. Although there are many variations, this style is one that is widely used. Law offices often have preformatted templates they require their attorneys and paralegals to use when researching a client's case, but they all include the following elements.

The first component is the **heading,** which describes who wrote the memo, to whom it was written, what it is about, and the date. The next element is the **questions presented section**, which should contain a balanced and understandable statement of the legal questions you will answer in the memo.

The **brief answer section** provides a **short answer** to each of the questions presented above it. Following the short answer section is the **statement of facts**, containing a formal and objective description of the legally significant facts in the problem. Next is the **discussion,** which is the heart of the memo. It is divided into segments according to the issues and sub-issues presented by the problem.

Lastly comes the **conclusion,** which is a longer, slightly different version of the brief answer in which you describe how you resolved the problem and the questions presented by the problem. We were taught to always make sure that our conclusion matches our short answer section in terms of predicted outcome.

To summarize, here are the elements of an office memorandum:

1. Heading;
2. Questions Presented;
3. Short Answer;
4. Statement of Facts;
5. Discussion; and
6. Conclusion.

Again, like all the previous information I have given you, we spent most of our first semester going over all of the above elements before actually writing an actual memo. You will be ahead of the game if you have this general background information before starting law school.

The Legal Brief

Another major undertaking for my second semester of Legal Research and Writing was a legal brief. The **brief** is the formal document a lawyer uses both to convince the court that his client's position is sound and to persuade the court to adopt that position. A brief is different than a memo in that, while the former overtly argues a case, the latter is a narrative that discusses the facts of a case in a strategic manner meant to *covertly* persuade the court to the plaintiff's argument. The brief is a legal document submitted to opposing counsel and a judge or panel of judges, such as in appellate courts, while the office memo is written to other attorneys, usually co-counsel or lawyers within the same law firm, to develop a legal strategy in preparation for a trial and/or other venues of arbitration.

Our professor stressed to us that legal advocacy and interpretation of the law can often turn into long-winded, complicated writing, which should be avoided. Instead he told us to make arguments that get to the point right away, using details when necessary. The "Rule of 3" is to be *clear, concise,* and *engaging* when summarizing the facts of the case and the legal reasoning behind your arguments in a legal brief.

An appellate brief contains many elements, including the title page, statement of the case, summary of argument, argument, conclusion, index, and finally an appendix. Within the above sections the attorney writing the brief will also include the questions presented, authorities cited, lower court opinions, jurisdiction, constitutional provisions, statutes, regulations, and rules involved that prove the attorney's position is the right one.

During our second semester of Legal Research and Writing we were paired up with a partner and asked to write an appellate brief. Then we participated in a "moot court" competition at school where we presented our briefs in front of a panel of judges formed by past alumni, judges, and lawyers from the surrounding legal community.

The set of facts we were given to work with dealt with areas involving constitutional law, civil procedure, criminal law, and criminal procedure. The specific issue in the fact pattern was whether a person had been deprived of his or her Fourteenth Amendment substantive due process rights in the context of a high-speed police pursuit.

It is not within the scope of this book to go into the detailed fact pattern or the brief itself (inasmuch as the brief my partner and I wrote ended up being eighteen pages long.) In addition, there are a number of different formats required by the various courts depending on the purpose of the brief. It would be extremely difficult to give examples of these here, but various types of briefs can be found on a number of court websites, including that of the United States Supreme Court.

Needless to say, I was terrified as to how I was going to possibly write the above brief and at the same time study for the rest of my second semester classes. Yet I did survive and so can you. Again, the key to a successful first year of law school is organization and efficiency—skills that will also aid you well throughout your legal career. Let's now move onto the third part of this book which will help you survive and thrive by preparing outlines and reducing stress through yoga.

PART III

C is for Class Outlines and Survival Skills

CHAPTER 13

The Art of the Outline

THERE'S NO SURE thing when it comes to acing final exams, but preparing good, condensed outlines is half the battle. You are probably already a good note taker, but you need to stretch those skills to study the right way for final exams and see the big picture of each class. As we discussed earlier, to survive you need to be able to recognize certain fact patterns on a final, and easily spot the issues involved. So, organizing your notes in a way that aids recall is crucial. That's where the well-crafted outline comes in.

I actually created two different outlines for each class: a short version and a long version. As you will see when reviewing the "short" outlines provided in the appendix of this book, the word short is a bit of a misnomer, as they are still fairly long. Think of these skeletal documents as big-picture, fill-in-the-blanks outlines, perfect for adding in the rules of law in your mind and testing your memory before finals. Much of my outlines actually came from important concepts garnered from my case briefs.

The second type of outline I recommend is a longer version of your own creation, packed with synopses of key rules, concepts, and relevant cases. Some of my lengthier outlines wound up being at least twenty-five pages, so, for the sake of brevity and conservation of trees, they are not included in this book.

Caveat: please do not rely on the outlines in this book alone when studying; instead, rely on the information you learn from your individual professors and include their specific teachings in your notes. The outlines included in this book are based on my own personal experience; as stated earlier, different professors teach the law in different ways and you should ultimately rely on what your professor is teaching when formulating your own outlines.

So, what do you do with the outlines in this book? For your convenience, they are available for download at our website, www.abclawschooldiary.com. I recommend reviewing each relevant outline before your first class to familiarize yourself with the concepts and get a head start grasping how the class might be organized. You can use these outlines as the basis for yours, filling in and adding along the way. Or, you can use them as a temperature check to see if your big picture matches mine on these basic, critical concepts.

It doesn't matter what type of outline you use as long as it covers the basic rules of law you're studying. The most important thing is that you understand your own outline, and that it helps you organize your thinking for your final exam. Another bonus of effective outlines is that you can use them for your bar review study when the time comes at the end of your third year. My outlines are meant to show you one way to organize all the information from your classes into a general, broad framework and give you hope that the massive, overwhelming amount of information directed your way *can* be made into something manageable.

How do you eat an elephant? One bite at a time.

CHAPTER 14

Stress Reduction for Law Students Through Yoga

In this chapter...

- ✓ Benefits of yoga
- ✓ What is yoga?
- ✓ Yoga and the law
- ✓ 5-minute daily yoga routine
- ✓ Styles of yoga

THE STRESS AND anxiety caused by adjusting to the rigors of the academic workload during the first year of law school can manifest in physical ways, leaving you feeling emotionally, mentally, and physically drained. Not only are students faced with the intense pressure of surviving this stressful time, but also with the demands of the fast-paced technological society in which we live.

Benefits of Yoga

Stress often results in physical tension in the body, as you've no doubt noticed. Practicing yoga can reduce stress levels by healing and cleansing the body and mind. Doing some simple yoga stretches and twists, combined with deep breathing, can help to loosen up tight muscles, stretch the spine, and relieve stress on the discs and joints. Furthermore, yoga helps to build a positive mental outlook, which helps when faced with stressful situations (like law school!). In essence, yoga gives you the tools to transform stress into positive energy. With a clearer mind, law students will be able to more easily sift through the voluminous legal cases they are assigned to read during the first year and beyond.

Besides easing stress, there are many other benefits of practicing yoga which include:

1. Building balance and flexibility;
2. Developing discipline;
3. Increasing coordination and strength;
4. Better concentration and focus;
5. Boosting self-confidence;
6. Toning internal glands and organs;
7. Promoting calmness;
8. Helping with other sports;
9. Heightening body-awareness and self-control; and
10. Is a non-competitive form of exercise, suitable for people of all ages, sizes, and athletic abilities.

In sum, practicing yoga is an ideal way for students to naturally unwind and obtain physical activity at the same time. Yoga nourishes the mind, body, and spirit, and paves the way for a life-long tradition of health and fitness, which will last way past that first year of law school. I can attest to this as I started practicing yoga over thirty-four years ago while in law school, and still maintain a daily practice to this day!

What is Yoga?

So, what exactly is yoga? It is an ancient science of the mind, body, and spirit developed in India nearly five thousand years ago. Yoga includes stretching exercises, mindfulness, and breathing techniques. As modern as it is ancient, yoga has become one of the most widely practiced exercise systems in the world. People engage in yoga not only for its physical benefits, but also to feel at peace with themselves.

Yoga is a modern-day tool to achieve peace, serenity, and well-being. In addition, this Eastern practice offers wide-ranging physical health benefits such as lowering blood pressure, reducing neck and back pain, promoting a healthy weight, and lowering the risk of heart disease. Hatha yoga, an ancient form that emphasizes physical postures, can improve cognitive function, boosting focus, and memory. What law student doesn't want that?!

Yoga and the Law

Some people, however, associate yoga with religion because it originated as an off-shoot of Hinduism; for instance, in *Sedlock v. Baird*, 35 Cal.App.4th 874 (2015), a civil rights lawsuit was filed by a family who claimed yoga promoted Hinduism and inhibited

Christianity. They tried to block Encinitas Union School District from teaching yoga as an alternative to traditional gym classes. The California appeals court upheld the ruling of the district court that the yoga classes in question did not violate students' rights. This case deals with an area of constitutional law; namely freedom of religion under the California Constitution.

The court said that, in deciding state establishment clause challenges, California's courts are guided by federal establishment clause rulings. Thus, the court analyzed the yoga program under the so-called *Lemon* test, from the 1971 U.S. Supreme Court's decision in *Lemon v. Kurtzman*, 403 U.S. 602 (1971). We'll talk more about the Lemon test in my Constitutional Law outline.

Under that test, a challenged government program must have a secular purpose, the program's primary purpose must not advance or inhibit religion, and it must not be excessively entangled with religion. The court assumed Ashtanga yoga was affiliated with the Hindu religion, but it said the district's program passed all three prongs of the *Lemon* test. Under the critical advancement prong, the district's yoga program did not advance Hinduism because it was "devoid of any religious, mystical, or spiritual trappings."

The three-judge panel of California's Fourth District Court of Appeal, based in San Diego, unanimously ruled that the yoga program of the Encinitas Union School District did not violate the state constitution's prohibition against government establishment of religion, stating "we see nothing in the content of the district's yoga program that would cause a reasonable observer to conclude that the program had the primary effect of either advancing or inhibiting religion."

The reason I am including a discussion of this case here is because I want to show you how the areas of law you study during your first year of law school pertain to current cases being tried in court. Also, I wanted to make the point that contemporary yoga is commonly practiced in the United States for reasons that are entirely distinct from religious ideology.

5-Minute Daily Yoga Routine

You're probably thinking that you don't have time to add yoga to your day, but that's not true. All it takes is five minutes to access the mental and physical benefits of yoga with a simple daily routine you can practice on your own while in law school. Unlike other exercise programs, yoga works on both the inside as well as outside of your body. A growing number of research studies have shown that the practice of Hatha Yoga can improve not only strength and flexibility but also may help to control blood pressure, respiration and heart rate, and metabolic rate. For example, a specific pose may not only strengthen your arms and legs, but may also work on internal organs and glands for proper functioning. Thus, by doing yoga you are literally giving your entire body an external and internal workout!

Everyone has a differing degree of flexibility; hence it is important to keep in mind while doing yoga that attention to form, breath, and focus are much more important than your range of motion. Just like the law books in the library, there are potentially an infinite amount of yoga poses; hence, the purpose of the ensuing yoga routine is only to give you a set of short and simple exercises to supplement a more in-depth practice.

While practicing the following 12 poses, it is important to focus on your breath. Breathing in and out through the nose can reduce stress. In stressful times, one tends to breathe rapidly, which can lead to increased anxiety. In contrast, slowing down the breath by inhaling and exhaling through the nose can help calm the body. Nasal breathing, as compared to mouth breathing, gets more oxygen into the lungs and can help prevent hyper-ventilation and the fight-or-flight response.

The following routine can be practiced in about five minutes, and contains **warming-up poses** (which increase blood flow to the major muscles and boost respiratory and heart rates), **standing poses** (which help develop greater strength, stamina, flexibility, and balance), **floor poses** (which strengthen the spine) and **winding down poses** (which help to unwind and relax the body.) For your convenience, a one-page summary of this special five-minute routine is included at the end of the book and also on www.abclawschooldiary.com. Pick a quiet place to practice yoga and try not to eat a big meal right before doing the poses. This is because many of the postures twist across glands and organs.

By doing this short yoga routine, you will not only achieve a stronger and more supple body and spine, but also will improve your physical and mental well-being. Always work within your own range of limits and abilities, and if you have any medical concern, talk with your doctor before practicing yoga and/or these poses.

Child's Pose

Let's begin with **Child's Pose,** (or *Balasana*). This posture helps your body to relax, clears your mind, and relieves back pain. If you have a current or recent knee injury, you should avoid this pose until consulting with your doctor.

Another option to start your yoga practice is to stand tall with your feet firmly planted on the ground. Bring your arms alongside your body, with your palms facing outward. Take at least five deep breaths in and out through your nose before moving on to the Cat/Cow Pose to be discussed next.

To do Child's Pose, kneel down onto the back of your heels and simply fold your upper body onto your thighs. Try to touch your forehead to the floor, with your arms long and extended, palms facing down. For a deeper relaxation, bring your arms back to rest alongside your thighs with your palms facing up. Take five deep breaths in and out through your nose in this position as you focus on why you are doing yoga today. Are you wanting a simple stretch or do you want a more vigorous workout? Everyday your body is different, and so is your energy level. Once you decide how you want to approach the following exercises, it is time to move on.

Cat/Cow Pose

Let's move on to the **Cat/Cow Pose** (*Marjaryasana/Bitilasana*). This yoga posture warms up your spine, and prepares it for the later postures. Get on your hands and knees, with your hands directly under your shoulders and your knees under your hips. With your arms straight and strong, round your spine by tucking your chin into your chest and holding in your stomach. This should be done while exhaling through your nose. Now inhale through your nose and straighten your spine, with your head facing down and your neck loose and relaxed. Repeat this sequence twice before moving on.

Downward Facing Dog Pose

From Cat/Cow Pose, tuck your toes behind you and straighten your arms out in front of you as you push back into **Downward Facing Dog** (*Adho Mukha Svanasana*). This posture not only releases tension in the upper spine and neck, but also lengthens the spine. Plus, it strengthens the hamstrings and arms.

While in this pose, try to keep your arms straight as you stretch your shoulders and head downward. Your weight should be evenly distributed between your hands and heels. The focus is to stretch your back fully; hence, you want to work on bringing your heels to the floor without straining your calves or Achilles tendons. Stretch and breathe in and out through your nose for at least three to five deep breaths before slowly and gently lowering your knees to the floor to exit this posture.

Chair Pose

Come to a standing position with your feet together. Stand tall and inhale as you raise your arms perpendicular to the floor. Exhale and bend your knees, trying to keep your thighs parallel to the floor. **Chair Pose (*Utkatasana*)** tones the entire body, particularly the thighs and ankles. It also stretches the Achilles tendons, shins, and shoulders.

Warrior II Pose

Warrior II (*Virabhadrasana II*) is a simple but powerful pose that is great for leg and core strength. It also builds stamina and concentration, as well as developing balance and stability. Start by standing with your feet together. Next, spread your legs wide apart with your feet facing forward. Turn your right foot out so it is at a 90-degree angle with your toes pointing away from your body; to maintain stability and balance, turn your left foot in slightly.

Stretch your arms out to your side, keeping them straight with your palms facing the ground. Your arms should be in line with your shoulders. Turn your head and look towards your right hand, focusing on your fingertips. If you have neck problems, avoid turning your head; instead continue to look straight ahead.

Bend your right knee and relax your shoulders as you breathe in and out through your nose in this position for around 5-10 seconds. To perform this posture on the other side, simply repeat the steps above, this time turning your left foot out to 90 degrees while bending your left knee and looking towards your left hand.

Tree Pose

Tree Pose (*Vrksasana*) is a standing balancing posture which has many benefits including developing muscle tone, coordination, strength, agility, and mental concentration.

Begin by standing up straight, and then slowly shift your weight to your right leg. Bending your left leg, clasp your left ankle with your left hand and place your left foot on the inside of your right thigh, either above or below your knee. Your left knee will extend out to the side. Focus on a point which is not moving in the distance, and slowly bring your hands to prayer position in front of your chest. Take three to five deep breaths in and out through your nose. You can also try to release your hands from prayer position and bring both your arms over your head for a more challenging variation.

There are always ways to adapt poses to your current abilities. For instance, if you are unsteady in Tree Pose you can practice this posture with your back against a wall or placing your fingertips on the back of a chair. Remember, it is the journey, not the destination, that counts when practicing yoga.

Cobra Pose

Cobra Pose (*Bhujangasana*) strengthens your spine and increases flexibility. It also stretches the muscles in the shoulders, chest and abdominals and helps to prevent low back pain. To begin, lie on your stomach, and bend your elbows close to your side. Keeping your elbows in this position, gently lift your chest and head up, keeping your legs straight behind you. Those who are very stiff can benefit from practicing Cobra while standing, with their hands placed against a wall. If you have a recent back or wrist injury, you should avoid this pose until consulting with your doctor.

Bow Pose

To do **Bow Pose** (*Dhanurasana*), lie on your stomach, like in **Cobra**, and then bend both of your knees. Grab hold of your ankles and lift your body off the ground. At first it may be difficult to lift the upper thighs away from the floor, but trust in the process. Your body will open up in time with practice. Also, if it is too challenging to grab your ankles, try looping a strap around your ankles and hold onto the ends of the strap instead.

This posture stretches out the chest and shoulders and is an excellent exercise for law students who sit hunched over their laptops or desks all day. It is also a great preparation for more challenging backbends. Not only does Bow Pose open up and stretch the front of the body, but also strengthens the muscles of the back of the body as well. This pose is a great antidote for stress and fatigue.

Reclining Pigeon Pose

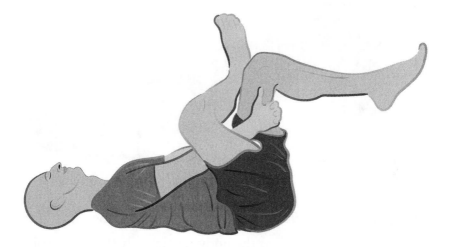

Reclining Pigeon Pose (*Supta Kapotasana*) is a modification of the classic pigeon pose which is done in a lunge position. This stretch helps ease tight hips and also is a great preventative stretch for the knees.

Lie on your back with your knees bent and the soles of your feet on the floor. Next, cross your right foot over your left knee, with your right knee sticking out to the side and your right foot flexed. Reach behind the hamstring on your left leg and hug it toward your chest. Keep your head flat on the floor by tucking your chin down. Hold this pose from 15 seconds to 2 minutes before switching sides.

Bridge Pose

Bridge Pose (*Setu Bandhasana*) is a backward bending pose which energizes and opens the body, particularly the upper spine and chest area. This posture also builds core and lower body strength and stimulates the endocrine and nervous systems.

Begin by lying on your back with your knees bent and feet hip distance apart. Your arms should be at your sides with your palms facing downward. Take a deep inhale through your nose, and on the exhale, lift your pelvis up as high as comfortable. Your weight should be evenly distributed between your shoulders and feet, with your chin pulling into your chest and your head on the floor. Take at least three to five deep breaths in this position, making sure that your stomach is relaxed as you work on lengthening your spine.

Seated Twist Pose

Begin by sitting on the floor with your legs extended out in front of you. Place your hands on the floor alongside your hips. Bend your right knee and place your right foot on the ground outside of your left thigh. Turn your torso to the right and take your right hand to the ground behind you, as you take your left arm outside of your right thigh. Inhale deeply to lengthen your spine, and on the exhale twist a little deeper. Breathe in and out through your nose for at least three deep breaths before switching sides.

This **Seated Twist Pose (*Arda Matsyendrasana*)** increases the flexibility and mobility of the pelvis, shoulders and joints. It also tones internal glands and organs by twisting across your kidney, liver and spleen. When you release the pose, fresh blood and oxygen flow to those parts of the body.

Easy Seated Twist Pose

If this pose is too much for you at first, you can begin with **Easy Seated Twist Pose** (*Parivrtta Sukhasana*). Begin with your legs crossed and arms resting at your sides. Next, take your right hand to the ground behind you and your left hand to your right knee. Take a big inhale to lengthen through your spine, then use your hands to twist your torso to the right.

Corpse Pose

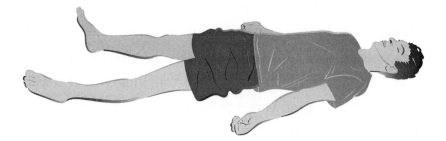

Corpse Pose (*Savasana*) is important to include at the end of your yoga practice, as it allows the body to process the new information it has received during the yoga session. It rejuvenates the body, mind and spirit while reducing stress and tension. Though it may seem like an easy pose, it can be quite difficult as the ability to lie completely still while being in the present moment takes a lot of practice and patience. However, the active, physically demanding poses leading up to it prepare you to release the mental chatter and surrender your body to a state of conscious rest.

To do Corpse Pose, lie on your back with your legs straight and arms at your sides. Rest your hands on the side of your body with your palms up, letting your feet drop open. Close your eyes, letting your breath occur naturally. Allow your body to feel heavy on the ground as you consciously release any tension from every part of your body. Relax your face as you allow peace and silence to take over. This may be the only time in your busy day that you can be alone and completely in the moment with no distractions or worries. Stay in this posture for 2 to 5 minutes to seal in the benefits of the poses you just practiced.

I like to listen to music when I practice yoga, and for this final resting posture I pick a new age classical song. You can also cover your eyes with a washcloth or eye pillow to keep the light out.

To exit Corpse Pose, first wiggle your fingers and toes as you roll over and gently press yourself into a comfortable seated position. Try to carry the peace and stillness of this posture throughout the rest of your day.

Styles of Yoga

There are many styles of yoga to choose from, and the list below are but some of the choices available to the yoga practitioner. You can search for yoga classes in your area at www.yogafinder.com.

1. **Hatha** is the umbrella term for all physical postures of yoga.
2. **Iyengar** focuses on alignment as well as detailed and precise movement.
3. **Kundalini** focuses on your core and breathing, with fast moving postures and breathing exercises.
4. **Ashtanga** involves a physically demanding sequence of poses and is not meant for the beginner.
5. **Vinyasa** is the most athletic yoga style which involves breath and movement and flowing from one pose to another.

6. **Hot yoga** features a sequence of set poses practiced in a sauna-like room.
7. **Yin yoga** is a slow-paced style of yoga with seated poses held for longer periods of time.
8. **Restorative yoga** focuses on body relaxation.
9. **Anusara yoga** focuses on alignment, but with more focus on the mind-body-heart connection.

For thousands of years yoga has kept muscles and joints running smoothly, toned internal organs, increased circulation, quieted the mind, and helped manage pain. I hope that you will try yoga during your law school career to keep your body aligned and balanced and your mind sharp and focused. And, don't forget: For your convenience, a one-page summary of this special five-minute routine is included at the end of the book and also on www.abclawschooldiary.com.

CHAPTER 15

Go Forth and Conquer

PHEW! WE TOUCHED on a lot in this diary, didn't we? I know you're not a legal know-it-all (yet) regarding all the complicated rules of law covered in each standard first year law school class. But, I do hope you've come away from this book with a greater awareness of what constitutes the body of law and picked up tips and tricks for prepping and studying for class, final exams and the bar. Understanding what is expected of you during that year is the first step toward a successful pursuit of your law career. Congratulations on taking it!

Let's see if we can tie everything together now in review. The traditional method of teaching law is the **case method,** which focuses on the professor's role in provoking students into a higher level of thinking through reading and analyzing case law found in the various class textbooks. **Case Law,** as we have seen, is derived from actual lawsuits, rather than just from statutes or codes. In your **Legal Research and Writing** class, you learn how to find both case law as well as laws derived from statutes and codes. In this course, you also learn how to write a memo and a brief, learn the basics of researching, and present an oral argument to a panel of volunteer judges. Many practicing attorneys say that this was their most useful and practical class in law school.

The **Torts** and **Contracts** classes teach you *what* lawyers do in civil court, while **Civil Procedure** teaches you *how* they do it. Procedural classes are helpful both in practice and on the bar examination. **Criminal Procedure** is also a procedural class and addresses the adjudication processes of **Criminal Law**. **Evidence** is to the law what anatomy is to medicine. This course, typically taught during one's second or third year of law school, is an in-depth examination of the rules governing the admissibility or exclusion of evidence at trial. I included a discussion of this class in my diary because Evidence is one of the subjects tested on the bar examination.

Another standard law school class that the vast majority of first year law students across the country take is **Real Property**. Like so much law in the United States, the laws governing the purchase, possession, and sale of property often date back to the English system of common law. Lastly, **Constitutional Law** classes deal with the different branches of government and their powers, as well as free speech and fundamental rights.

I hope that you can now see how interconnected all the courses are to one another and how you will use them on a daily basis once you're a practicing attorney. For instance, Criminal Law and Civil Procedure give an attorney guidelines for the procedural rules regarding his or her cases, and Legal Research and Writing gives an attorney the tools to look up the law and write any sort of legal papers on behalf of his or her client. Both **substantive** law and **procedural** law work together to ensure that in a criminal or civil case, the appropriate laws are applied and proper procedures are followed when bringing a case to trial.

Substantive law consists of written statutory rules passed by the legislature that govern how people behave. These rules, or laws, define crimes, set forth punishments, and define our rights and responsibilities as citizens. There are elements of substantive law in both criminal and civil law, and the key first year classes that help an attorney with the substantive law are Torts, Contracts, Real Property, and Constitutional Law.

The knowledge I obtained and the thinking processes I learned during that first year of law school served me well far beyond the final exams. The law is an important part of our society as it continues to set up rules of conduct that guide our actions in our daily lives. Despite the explosion of data and rise of virtual technology, it provides a basic structure to regulate our behavior and protect our basic rights. I hope that by reading *The ABCs of Law School*, you now feel more confident with the process of preparing for law school. By learning what to expect from your first year, as well as how to master it through effective organization, strategic study skills, and a conscious effort at stress reduction, you will have the tools to survive and thrive!

I wish you good luck in your law pursuit, as you go forth and conquer!

APPENDIX/OUTLINES

Torts

To refresh your memory, a tort is a harmful act which a person might be held legally responsible for under civil law. Before we get to the good stuff (the outline), I'd like to explain how the outline for Torts is organized differently from my other outlines.

I became good friends with a second-year law student who suggested that I use a special mnemonic device when examining any tort problem on a final exam. It was **EDD**, or "Every **D**og has its **D**ay."

The first **E** stands for **Elements**. The **D** stands for **Damages** and the second **D** stands for **Defenses**. Thus, on a Torts final exam question you would read the fact pattern and first determine what kind of tort occurred (either intentional, negligent or strict liability).

Once you identify the type of tort, it's time for every dog to have its day! The three **Elements** of every tort action are the **existence of a legal duty** from the defendant to the plaintiff, a **breach of that duty,** and **damages** as a proximate cause. Hence, if a fact pattern on a Torts final exam dealt with the intentional torts of assault and battery, the analysis would begin with whether the defendant owed a legal duty to the plaintiff, whether that duty was breached and finally whether there were any damages suffered as a consequence of the defendant's actions. Your answer would evolve through a discussion of the specific elements of an assault and battery and whether those elements are present in the specific fact pattern at hand. An **assault** is any intentional, unexcused act which creates in another person a reasonable apprehension of immediate harmful contact. A **battery**, on the other hand, is any unexcused, harmful, or offensive physical contact intentionally performed.

Once the elements of a specific tort have been discussed, the next thing to focus on during the final exam are the **damages**. There can be either **punitive** (damages awarded as a punishment, in excess of the actual harm suffered), **compensatory** (monetary compensation that the law awards to one who has been injured by the action of another), or **nominal** damages. Nominal damages are a trivial sum awarded to vindicate the plaintiff's claim where no recoverable loss can be established.

The last area to cover for every torts problem is **defenses**. There are specific defenses we studied in depth concerning strict liability torts, intentional torts, as well as negligent acts. Thus, the mnemonic **EDD** (**E**very **D**og has its **D**ay) can help you to organize your thoughts and write cohesive essays at Torts final exam time.

Like we discussed in chapter 13, I actually used two outlines for my Torts class, as well for as my other classes; a short version and a long version. The one that follows is the short version, which briefly lists the categories of torts under specific headings and is organized according to the EDD learning device. This is the only class outline that is oriented according to a mnemonic. So, think of the outlines here as your "fill-in-the-blanks" outlines, perfect for adding in the rules of law in your mind and testing your memory before finals. The second kind of outline is the long version, packed with synopses of all the rules we studied in connection with the specific types of torts. Creating those outlines, my friend, is up to you!

Caveat: do not rely on the outlines in this book and these outlines alone; instead always rely on the information you learn from your individual professors. This outline is just meant to show you one way to organize all the information from your classes into a general, broad framework. And, all of these outlines are available for download on our website, www.abclaw-schooldiary.com.

Torts Outline

I. Torts: **E**very **D**og has its **D**ay

   A. **E**lements of a Specific Tort

      1. Kinds of Torts

         a. Intentional Torts

            1.) Against Persons

               a.) False Imprisonment

               b.) Assault

               c.) Battery

               d.) Intentional Infliction of Emotional Distress

            2.) Against Property

               a.) Trespass to Land

               b.) Conversion

               c.) Trespass to Chattels

         b. Negligence

            1.) Proof of Negligence

               a.) Duty

               b.) Causation

               c.) Breach of Duty

               d.) Damages

            2.) Gross Negligence must be proved

               a.) Auto guest statutes

            3.) Negligence need not be proved in some specific instances

               a.) Violation of a safety statute

               b.) *Res Ipsa Loquitur.*

Negligence of the alleged wrongdoer may be inferred from the mere fact that the accident happened.

4.) Standards of Care

    a.) Objective Standard: Based on a reasonable, ordinary, prudent person (**TARM** – **T**he **A**verage **R**easonable **M**an).

    b.) There are also different standards of care for specific types of people:

        1.] Insane persons

        2.] Children

        3.] Physically handicapped people

        4.] Intoxicated persons

        5.] Professional

        6.] Extremely low intelligence

c. Strict Liability (liability regardless of fault):

    1.) Animals

        a.) Different rules for dangerous v. domestic animals

    2.) Ultrahazardous Activities

d. Miscellaneous Torts

    1.) Landowners and Occupiers

    2.) Products Liability

        a.) Strict Liability

        b.) Warranty

            1.] Express

            2.] Implied

c.) Negligence

3.) Nuisance:

A wrong arising from unreasonable or unlawful use of property to the annoyance or damage of another or the public.

a.) Private v. Public Nuisance

b.) Remedies

1.] Legal: Money Damages

2.] Equity: Injunctive Relief

4.) Defamation

a.) Forms of Defamation

1.] Libel (written)

2.] Slander (oral)

b.) Elements of Defamation

1.] Defamatory Statements

2.] Publication

3.] Fault

4.] Actual Damages

c.) Remedies

1.] Compensatory

2.] Mitigation of Damages

5.) Misuse of Legal Procedure

a.) Malicious Prosecution

b.) Wrongful Civil Proceeding

c.) Abuse of Process

6.) Misrepresentation

a.) Intentional

b.) Negligent

7.) Interference with Advantageous
   Relationships
   a.) Interference with Family Relations
   b.) Injurious Falsehood
   c.) Interference with an Existing Contract
   d.) Interference with Prospective Advantage

e. Special Issues
   1.) Statutes of Limitations
      a.) May run from date of injury; OR
      b.) May run from date injury should have
         been known; OR
      c.) May run from last exposure to product
   2.) Vicarious Liability
   3.) Multiple Defendants

B. Damages:

An award, typically money, paid to a person as
compensation for loss or injury.

1. Compensatory
2. Nominal
3. Punitive

C. Defenses

1. Defenses to Intentional Torts
   a. Consent:
      1.) Implied
      2.) Express
   b. Self-defense
   c. Defense of Others
   d. Defense of Property

e. Necessity

    1.) Public

    2.) Private

f. Shopkeeper's Privilege

g. Government Entities

h. Nonfeasance

i. Authority of Law

j. Recovery of Property

2. Defenses to Negligence

    a. Necessity

        1.) Last clear chance is a defense to contributory negligence

    b. Comparative Negligence: Proportionate sharing between plaintiff and defendant of responsibility for injury to the plaintiff (Pure Form v. 50 percent Rule).

    c. Assumption of Risk

    d. Immunity

        1.) Charitable

        2.) Family

        3.) Governmental

    e. Statutes of Limitations: Any law that fixes the time within which parties must take judicial action to enforce their rights.

3. Defenses to Strict Liability

    a. Scope of Risk

    b. Assumption of Risk

    c. Abnormal Sensitivity

      d. Comparative Negligence

      e. Contributory Negligence

4. Defenses to Products Liability

      a. Strict Liability Defenses

          1.) Assumption of Risk

          2.) Unforeseeable Abnormal Use

          3.) Comparative Negligence

      b. Warranty Defenses

          1.) Disclaimer

          2.) Timeliness

          3.) Comparative Negligence

          4.) Assumption of Risk

          5.) Limitations on Liability

      c. Negligent Products Liability Defenses

          1.) All the same defenses are used as in an ordinary negligence case.

5. Defenses to Nuisance

      a. Contributory Negligence

      b. Assumption of Risk

      c. "Coming to the Nuisance"

      d. Governmental Authority

      e. Others are Liable

6. Defenses to Defamation

      a. Truth

      b. Privileges

          1.) Qualified v. Absolute Privileges

      c. Consent

II. Tort Reform
    A. Limitation of Damages
    B. Manufacturing Defects
    C. Design Defects
    D. Information Defects
    E. Defenses
    F. Settlement and Apportionment
    G. Damages

Extra Credit:

As you can see from this brief outline of my entire year of Torts, there are many concepts you need to know to do well on your final exam. The above outline served me well as a way to test my memory and understanding of tort law. My second outline contained the same basic skeletal structure but was filled in with all the rules of law on the items covered, as well as some relevant case names.

For instance, I added *MacPherson v. Buick Motor Co.*, 111 N.E. 1050 (1916) to my longer outline under the section dealing with negligence and products liability. In this landmark tort case, MacPherson was injured when the wheel on his car collapsed. Buick claimed that it wasn't liable because it didn't manufacture the wheel. In a majority opinion, Justice Benjamin Cardozo held that a plaintiff's recovery cannot be foreclosed just because he or she didn't have a contract directly with the party that made the faulty part. This New York Court of Appeals decision expanded the classification of **inherently dangerous products** and eliminated the requirement of a contractual relationship between the parties in cases involving defective products that cause injury.

Legal Research & Writing Outline

The skeletal outline that follows offers a general understanding of what legal research is all about, not only for law students, but also for lawyers. It shows, in outline form, how a first year law student not only learns research tools, but also becomes familiar with accessing both print and electronic research materials. As with all my outlines, there are multiple specific rules and other tips which your teacher will teach you as you navigate the realm of legal research. Thus, this outline should not be relied upon as a substitute for a more comprehensive guide to finding sources of the law.

I. Categories of Authority:

Each jurisdiction's court uses various authorities to make a ruling on a case.

A. Primary Authority:

1. Law issued by a branch of government.
   a. Judicial Branch
      1.) Interprets a statute or constitution.
      2.) Makes laws through common law.
   b. Legislative Branch
      1.) Enacts laws.
   c. Executive/Administrative Branch
      1.) Issues rules or regulations to implement legislation.
      2.) President and state governors can issue executive orders.

2. Binding Authority:
   Lower courts must follow rulings of higher courts
   in their jurisdiction.
   a. Federal courts do not bind state courts except
      for U.S. Supreme Court on a federal issue.
3. Persuasive Authority:
   Court considers the reasoning of another court.
4. Primary Authority Research
   a. Appellate and Supreme Courts
      1.) Official (by courts) and Unofficial (by
         commercial publisher) reports
         a.) Most opinions of federal and state courts
            appear in National Reporter System
         b.) For Supreme Court, if official report
            of case exists, it must be cited, and it
            precedes an unofficial site.
      2.) Some federal trial court opinions are
         published.
         a.) State Court Case Reporters
            1.] Seven Regional Reporters (West
               Regional Reporter Series)
               a.] *North Eastern Reporter*: N.E.,
                  N.E.2d
               b.] *Atlantic Reporter*: A., A.2d, A.3d
               c.] *South Eastern Reporter*: S.E., S.E.
                  2d
               d.] *Southern Reporter*: So., So. 2d
               e.] *South Western Reporter*: S.W., S.W.
                  2d, S.W. 3d

    f.] *North Western Reporter*: N.W.,
    N.W. 2d

    g.] *Pacific Reporter*: P., P. 2d, P. 3d

 b. Organization of Reporter Cases

   1.) Jurisdiction:

   Cases from specific or several courts will be published together.

   2.) Geography:

   Several states are combined to include a regional area.

   3.) Subject Matter:

   Court opinions are reported in various loose-leaf services for that particular subject.

 c. Stages of Publication

   1.) Slip Opinion:

   Issued same day as court announces its opinion and available from online services or clerk of court.

    a.) Does not include summary of case, index, or other research aids.

    b.) Subject to further editing before it is published officially.

   2.) Advance Sheet:

   Paper-bound pamphlets containing recent decisions of cases from a jurisdiction. These will eventually be reprinted in subsequent bound

   3.) Bound Volume:

Table of cases in alphabetical order and according to state.

B. Secondary Authority

1. All other written expressions of law.
2. Court can use as basis for a decision.
3. Provides a basis for argument to change law.
4. Secondary Authority Research
   a. Attorney General Opinions:
   b. Persuasive advisory opinions which are not binding.
      1.) Restatements:
         Published by American Law Institute (ALI).
         a.) Attempt to codify common law.
         b.) Written by experts in particular field, setting forth what law is or should be.
         c.) Revised and published in new editions.
   c. Legal Periodicals
      1.) Research tool for cites to primary and secondary sources.

II. Foundation of the Legal System

A. Doctrine of *Stare Decisis:*

The following of rules or principles laid down in previous judicial decisions unless they contravene the ordinary principles of justice.

1. All courts are bound by their own earlier decisions *unless*:
   a. Reversed by a higher court; or

    b. If they are the highest deciding court, they decided to formally override their decision.

  2. All federal courts must follow United States Supreme Court decisions.

B. U.S. Constitution

  1. Publications:

    a. Official publication: U.S. Codes (U.S.C. or USC)

    b. Unofficial publications: U.S. Code Annotated (U.S.C.A. or USCA), and U.S. Code Service (U.S.C.S. or USCS)

C. State Constitutions

  1. Publications:

    a. Annotated codes;

    b. State or regional digests;

    c. Local law reviews;

    d. State encyclopedias; and

    e. Multi-volume loose-leaf set entitled *Constitutions of the United States: National and State.*

III. Federal Court Reporters

A. Supreme Court Decisions

  1. Official Reporter: *U.S. Reports*

  2. Unofficial versions include:

    a. *Supreme Court Reports*

    b. *U.S. Supreme Court Reports, Lawyers Edition,*

and *Lawyers Edition Second Series*

3. *United States Law Week:*

Two volume set loose-leaf reporter published by the Bureau of National Affairs.

    a. Volume 1 contains all U.S. Supreme Court actions.

    b. Volume 2 contains recent important federal and state court opinions, as well as:

        1.) Legal and administrative law highlights; and

        2.) Legal news and summaries.

B. Federal Appellate Court Decisions

1. *Federal Reporter, Federal Reporter 2d*, and *Federal Reporter 3d*

    a. Contains all circuit court of appeals decisions, as well as opinions of:

        1.) U.S. Court of Claims;

        2.) Temporary Emergency Court of Appeals; and

        3.) U.S. Court of Customs and Patent Appeals.

2. Federal District Court Decisions

    a. Federal Supplement, Federal Supplement 2d

        1.) Includes select trial court decisions.

        2.) Prior to 1933, Federal District Court opinions can be found in Federal Reporter and Federal Cases, along with appellate decisions prior to 1880.

3. Specialty Court Decisions

    a. Tax Court, Court of Claims, and Court of International Trade publish their own opinions.

b. Bankruptcy
1.) *West's Bankruptcy Reporter*
2.) *West's Bankruptcy Digest*

IV. Federal and State Statutes
A. Stages of Publication for Federal Statutes
1. Official:
   a. Slip Laws:
   The first official publication of an Act of Congress, known as a slip law, is prepared by the Office of the Federal Register and published individually in an unbound pamphlet.
   b. Session Laws:
   At the end of a congressional session, the slip laws are compiled into bound volumes called the *United States Statutes at Large* and called session laws.
3. Unofficial:
   Federal session laws are also published by West as *The United States Code Congressional & Administrative News* (U.S.C.C.A.N.) in print versions and online on Westlaw.com.

B. State Statutes
1. Each state publishes a set of statutes approved by the state legislature during the most recent session and signed by the governor. They are arranged chronologically and are also known as session laws.
2. Updating State Statutes

      a. Session Law Services

      b. Shepardize provision to find out whether statute repealed or amended

V. Administrative Law

A. Authority derived from the Executive branch of government

   1. Rule-making and adjudication

B. Sources of Federal Administrative Law

   1. *Federal Register*

   2. *Code of Federal Regulations* (CFR)

   3. Loose-leaf Services: Commerce Clearing House (CCH), Prentice Hall(P-H) and Bureau of National Affairs (BNA)

   4. Other Sources

      a. *Federal Yellow Book; Congressional Yellow Book*

      b. *Shepard's United States Administrative Citations*

   5. Presidential Documents

      a. *Federal Register* (FR or Fed. Reg.)

      b. United States Code Service (USCS)

      c. *US. Code Congressional and Administrative News* (U.S.C.C.A.N.)

C. Sources of State Administrative Law

   1. Some states publish regulations, state manuals, and weekly supplements, but the agency itself is the best source.

VI. Research Procedure
A. Identify Legal Issues
1. Search for authority that determines the legal issues in your fact situation.

B. Background
1. Use secondary sources for broad overview of general subject matter groupings.

C. Citations
1. *Uniform System of Citation The Bluebook*
2. *ALWD Guide to Legal Citation,* complied by Association of Legal Writing Directors

D. Locating Case Law
1. With Citation: Locate correct reporter using volume and page number in citation.
2. Without Citation:
    a. If you know name of case, you can search for it by:
        1.) Jurisdiction: Cases are listed in alphabetical order by plaintiff's name.
        2.) Searching in one of West's five related digests
            a.) *Federal Digest* through 1939
            b.) *Modern Federal Practice Digest* 1939-1961
            c.) *West's Federal Practice Digest 2nd* 1961-1975
            d.) *West's Federal Practice Digest 3rd* 1975-1983: Burgundy
            e.) *West's Federal Practice Digest 4th* 1983–present: Blue

3.) Defendant's name: Check defendant/
plaintiff table

4.) *Shepard's Acts and Cases by Popular Names,*
Federal and State

    b. If you don't know the name of the case:

1.) Check digest topic, words & phrases, or
digest's descriptive word index by subject

VII. Computer-Assisted Legal Research

A. Online Services

1. www.Westlaw.com and www.LexisNexis.com: most
widely used

2. Legal periodicals, congressional, and government
publications

B. Internet

1. Free information is available, but it is difficult
to filter through mass of information to locate
suitable, reliable material.

VIII. Other Useful Sources

A. Treatises

B. Legal Encyclopedias

C. American Law Reports (ALR): Annotated reports.

D. Practice and Procedure Books

1. State Continuing Legal Education (CLE)
Materials

2. Federal and State Civil and Criminal Procedure
Codes

E. Form Books

1. Supplements to Practice and Procedure Books

F. Dictionaries and Glossaries

IX. Shepardizing

A. Before citing a statute or case as authority:

1. Verify that it is still "good law," in that it has not been:
   a. Overruled;
   b. Modified; or
   c. Excessively criticized.
2. Find appropriate set of *Shepard's Citations*
   a. Print listings are in numerical order by volume and page number.
   b. Case law on LexisNexis can be searched by a number of parameters quickly.
3. *Shepard's* print version includes all citations for:
   a. Cases: state and federal
   b. Statutes
   c. Attorney general opinions
   d. American Law Reports (ALR) annotations
   e. Law reviews and other journals
   f. Legal texts
4. *Shepard's Citation Service* online can be found through LexisNexis.
   a. "Shepardize" button will provide a complete Shepardized report on the case instantaneously.
   b. Not all codes and case law in the print version are available online so sometimes print Shepardization is still necessary.
5. *Key-Cite*: Citation system from Westlaw

Contracts Outline

I. Contracts Overview

A. Basic definition of a contract:

A promise or set of promises which are enforceable under the law.

B. Common Law v. Uniform Commercial Code (UCC)

1. Article 2 of the UCC applies to transactions for the sale of goods (goods are defined as tangible, moveable property).

2. Most other contracts are covered by common law.

C. The Agreement Process:

This is the formation of a contract.

1. Offer
   a. Offeror: Person who makes the offer.
   b. Offeree: Person to whom the offer is made.
   c. There must be an intent to contract with definite terms.
   d. Offers v. Non-Offers
      1.) Opinions
      2.) Advertising
      3.) Inquiries and Quotes
      4.) Auctions
   e. Duration of Offer
   f. Termination of Offer
      1.) By Offeror
         a.) Revocation
         b.) Unilateral contract:

Generally the offer becomes irrevocable once offeree begins performance; mere preparation is not enough.

  2.) By Offeree

    a.) Rejection

    b.) Counter-Offer

    c.) By Operation of Law

2. Acceptance

 a. Common Law:

  Acceptance must mirror terms (Mirror Image Rule)

  1.) Bilateral v. unilateral contracts

    a.) Bilateral: Acceptance by return promise

    b.) Unilateral: Acceptance by return

  2.) Silence is NOT acceptance as an express contract is formed by words.

    a.) Exception: Silence may be acceptance if:

      1.] An "implied-in-fact" contract is formed by conduct;

      2.] Trade practice; or

      3.] Offeree takes benefit.

 b. Mailbox Rule

  1.) Acceptance is valid when sent.

  2.) Exception: Offer stipulates that acceptance is not effective until received.

3. Consideration

 a. Bargained for exchange:

  There is a benefit to promisor or detriment to promisee.

b. Adequacy of Consideration:
Generally courts do not review the adequacy of consideration as there is a presumption of fair bargaining between parties.
1.) Exception: False or nominal consideration.
c. Mutuality of Obligation
d. Substitution for Consideration
1.) Promissory Estoppel:
A legal principle that states that a promise is enforceable by law, even if made without consideration, when a promisor has made a promise to a promisee who then relies on that promise to his detriment.

D. Performance of a Contract

1. Conditions:
Occurrence or non-occurrence of an event which limits the duty to perform a contract, so that the failure of the condition discharges the liability of the promisor.
a. Express condition:
Created by agreement of the parties.
b. Constructive condition:
Imposed by law to do justice.
1.) Also called an "implied-in-law" contract.
c. Time of occurrence of conditions
1.) Condition Precedent:
Condition occurs before the duty of performance.

2.) Condition Concurrent:
Condition occurs at the moment of

3.) Condition Subsequent:
Occurrence of the condition after performance cuts off the existing duty to perform.

   d. Conditions of satisfaction

   e. Excuse of condition

     1.) Wrongful prevention, hinderance, and failure to cooperate

     2.) Waiver or election of a condition

     3.) Forfeiture

     4.) Divisibility

E. **Breach of Contract:**

Failure to perform any term of a contract, written or oral, without a legitimate excuse.

1. Material Breach
   a. Total Breach
   b. Partial Breach

2. Minor/Immaterial breach:
Failure to perform a duty that is not central to the contract.
   a. Factors to Consider
     1.) Extent of Performance
     2.) Delay in Performance
     3.) Willfulness or Negligence
     4.) Substantial Performance

3. Anticipatory Repudiation v. Prospective Inability to Perform

F. Remedies:

Compensation for harm caused by a breach.

1. Damages
   a. Expectancy Damages
      1.) The goal is to make the non-breaching party 'whole' by putting him or her in as good of a position as if the promise were performed.
      2.) General v. Consequential Damages
         a.) General Damages:
            Those damages arising naturally form the result of the breach.
         b.) Consequential Damages:
            Special damages allowed if both parties knew of them or if they were foreseeable.
      3.) Duty to Mitigate Damages:
         The non-breaching party must take steps to reduce the loss to the lowest sum possible.
   b. Reliance Damages:
      The measure of compensation given to a person who suffered an economic harm for acting in reliance on a party who failed to fulfill their obligation.
   c. Nominal Damages:
      These damages are symbolic for the purpose of establishing precedent or a cause of action. If there is no measurable, actual loss, the court will award $1 for technical breach.

d. Punitive Damages:

Purpose is to deter wrongdoers from similar conduct.

1.) These types of damages are awarded for the purpose of:

a.) Punishing fraud.

b.) Violating a fiduciary duty and acts of bad faith.

e. Liquidated (Stipulated) Damages

1.) The contract settles in advance what the damages will be.

2. Restitution:

The purpose of this equitable remedy is to restore to the plaintiff the value of a benefit unjustly conferred, regardless of the contract price.

a. This remedy is only available for a total breach of contract, *not* a partial breach.

3. Specific Performance:

Also an equitable remedy which mandates that the breaching party carry out the contractual duties or is enjoined from action.

a. It is only granted if a party's monetary damages are inadequate and is not a common remedy.

b. In Common Law, this remedy applies to the sale of land as well as the sale of unique goods.

G. Defenses to Duty to Perform:

When there is a valid defense, one or both parties do not have to perform the contract and their nonperformance is *not* a breach.

1. Legal Incapacity
   a. Minors
   b. Mentally infirm
2. Duress
3. Undue Influence
4. Misrepresentation of Material Fact
5. Mutual Mistake and Unilateral Mistake
6. Illegality
7. Unconscionability
8. Impossibility and Commercial Impracticability
9. Frustration of Purpose

H. Nonparties:

Those involved in a contract other than the offeree and offeror.

1. Third-Party Beneficiaries
2. Assignment and Delegation
3. Delegation

I. Issues Related to Writing

1. Statue of Frauds:

   This rule is intended to prevent fraud by requiring certain types of contracts be in writing to be enforceable.

   a. Promises to answer for the debt or duty of another.
   b. Contract not to be performed within one year from the making of it.
   c. Contracts to sell any interest in real property.

      d. Contracts not to be performed within the lifetime of the promisor.

      e. Contracts for the sale of goods over the statutory price ($500, UCC 2-201).

2. Parole Evidence Rule

      a. The parole evidence rule treats formal written documents created by parties as reflective of their true intentions regarding which terms are meant to be included in the contract.

         1.) Writing that is intended to be the final evidence of an agreement between the parties may not be contradicted or added to whether the document is complete or incomplete.

      b. The purpose of this rule is to prevent a party from introducing evidence of prior oral agreements that occurred before or while the agreement was being reduced to its final form in order to alter the terms of the existing contract.

J. Termination of Contracts

1. Performance:

      a. The performance of promises and duties discharges the rights and responsibilities in a contract.

2. Breach

3. Mutual Recission, or Recission by Agreement: A discharge of both parties from the obligations of a contract by a new agreement made after the

execution of the original contract but prior to its performance.

4. Accord and Satisfaction:

    The accord is an agreement substituting performance and the satisfaction is the performance.

5. Substituted Contract:

    The same parties to a contract may agree to replace an existing obligation with a new contract.

6. Account Stated:

    This is a statement between a creditor and debtor which settles the total amount of debt owed under a contract to the creditor.

    a. Novation:

        An agreement among all the parties to a contract which substitutes a new party and a brand-new contract is created.

Extra Credit:

It is also a good idea to add the names of landmark cases which illustrate the rule of law into your outline; I touched upon this in the section on my Torts outline. During your first year Contracts class you will encounter some of the most classic law school cases, including *Hawkins v. McGee*, 84 N.H. 114 (1929). This case made its way to popular culture, as it appears in the 1973 movie, *The Paper Chase*. It is often referred to as the "hairy hand" case. Hawkins's hand was scarred nine years earlier, and he went to Dr.

McGee to fix it. McGee promised a "one hundred percent good hand." He used skin from Hawkins' chest to repair the scar, but not only did it not work, but Hawkins' hand grew thick hair on it. This case is notable, not just for the hairy hand, but because the court used "expectancy" as the value of Hawkins' damages; namely, the value of a "one hundred percent good hand." I added this case into my longer Contracts outline under "Remedies for Breach of Contract and Expectancy Damages," as it is a leading case on damages in contract law.

Civil Procedure Outline

The law of civil procedure, although not covered on the bar examination, is one of the most important classes you will take as it contains the rules and procedures that lawyers use in their everyday practices, especially in litigation. Before diving in, a quick note: I endeavored to update this outline to the way that the law is currently taught, but it is primarily still based on what I learned back in law school.

I. Civil Procedure

A. United States Constitution (USC):

The USC created federal courts of limited jurisdiction (USC Art. III., Section 2).

B. *Federal Rules of Civil Procedure* (FRCP)

C. *United States Code Title 28* (28 USC)

D. Types of Jurisdiction:

Jurisdiction deals with whether a court has authority over a certain subject matter or individual.

1. Jurisdiction over the Person (Personal Jurisdiction)
   a. Five Elements
      1.) Activities must be systematic and continuous (*Helicoperos Nacionales de Colombia, SA v. Hall*, 466 U.S. 408 (1984)).
      2.) Activities must be purposely directed toward the forum state (*Asahi Metal Industry Company v. Superior Court*, 480 U.S. 102 (1987)).

3.) Defendant must purposefully avail himself or herself of the privileges of the forum state (*Hanson v. Denckla*, 357 U.S. 235 (1958)).

4.) Possibility of litigation must be foreseeable (*World-Wide Volkswagen Corporation v. Woodson*, 444 U.S. 286 (1980)).

5.) There must be a connection between the litigation, defendant, and forum state.

b. Substantive Due Process:

1.) Constitutional requirement that a defendant have certain minimum contacts with the forum state or territory in which the court sits in order for that court to exercise power over the defendant (*International Shoe Company v. Washington*, 326 U.S. 310, (1945)).

2. Jurisdiction over Property:

a. *In rem* Jurisdiction

b. *Quasi in rem* Jurisdiction

3. Subject Matter Jurisdiction:

a. Limited Jurisdiction

b. General Jurisdiction

4. Original Jurisdiction:

This type of jurisdiction governs the trial courts. These courts have the authority to hear the case first.

5. Appellate Jurisdiction:

The power of a higher court to review and change the decisions of lower courts.

6. Federal Jurisdiction:

District courts hear cases involving rights and obligations arising from the Constitution or federal law. Many federal courts are based on subject matter jurisdiction.

  a. Two ways a federal court can gain subject matter jurisdiction over a case:

    1.) If a federal question arises in the plaintiff's case, based on one or more of the following:

      a.) The United States Constitution (USC);

      b.) A treaty; or

      c.) A federal law.

    2.) Diversity of citizenship can give federal courts jurisdiction over cases arising between:

      a.) Citizens of different states;

      b.) A foreign country & citizens of a state or different states; or

      c.) Citizens of the state and citizens of a foreign country.

        1.] The amount in controversy must exceed $75,000 in diversity of citizenship cases.

        2.] Domicile for individuals:

          The most recent state where they

resided with intent to remain
indefinitely.

3.] Domicile for corporations:

The state of their incorporation and
the state of its principal place of
business.

a.] "Nerve Center" or "Place of
Activity Test":

Place where a company's principal
affairs of business are maintained.

I control
my company.

Then you also
control diversity
jurisdiction!

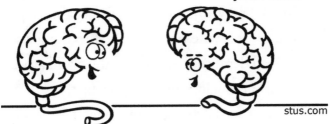

stus.com

Nerve Center Test

7. Concurrent Jurisdiction:

When two different courts have authority to hear
the same case.

8. Exclusive Jurisdiction:

When only one court has authority to hear a
particular case.

9. Supplemental Jurisdiction:

When a lawsuit consists of more than one claim
and the federal court has valid jurisdiction (either

diversity or federal question jurisdiction) over at least one of the claims.

10. Ancillary Jurisdiction:

A federal court may hear a claim normally outside of its subject-matter jurisdiction if the claim is substantially related to a second claim within the court's jurisdiction.

11. Pendent Claim Jurisdiction:

Jurisdiction of federal courts over nonfederal claims between parties litigating other matters properly before the court.

12. Pendent Party Jurisdiction:

A court may adjudicate a claim against a party who would otherwise not be subject to the jurisdiction of the federal courts, because the claim arose from a common nucleus of operative fact.

> *Note:* In 1990, Congress enacted the supplemental jurisdiction statute (28 U.S.C. § 1367), which largely codified, with certain distinctions, the former common law doctrines of pendent, ancillary, and pendent party jurisdiction. Prior to 1990, supplemental jurisdiction was governed by common law.

E. Venue, as opposed to jurisdiction, involves the particular geographic area within a judicial district where a suit should be brought (28 USC § 1391 and §§1392-1413).

1. Criminal Cases:
   a. Venue is usually the district or county where the crime was committed.
2. Civil Cases:
   a. Usually the district or county which is the residence of the principal defendant.
   b. Where a contract was executed or is to be performed, or where an accident took place.
3. Venue has to do with trying a suit in a district where the interests of justice as well as the convenience of the parties and witnesses is taken into consideration.

F. **Types of Courts**
   1. Trial Courts
      a. State Trial Courts
      b. Federal Trial Courts
   2. Appellate Courts
      a. State Appellate Courts
      b. Federal Appellate Courts
   3. Supreme Courts
      a. State Supreme Courts
      b. Federal: The Supreme Court

G. **Removal from State to Federal Court**
   1. Basis for removal
   2. Strictly at defendant's option.

H. **Law Applied by Federal Courts**
   1. State Law in Federal Court
      a. Erie Doctrine:

Federal courts in diversity actions must apply the substantive law of the state in which they sit (*Erie Railroad Co. v. Tompkins*, 304 U.S. 64 (1938)).

2. Federal Common Law

    a. Developed by federal courts rather than the courts of the various states. Only applicable if Congress has not repealed it.

I. Service of Process and Notice:

1. Commencing an Action (FRCP 3): Filing a Complaint with the Court

2. Summons (FRCP 4)

3. Issuance

4. Service

5. Waiving Service

6. Serving an Individual within a Judicial District of the U.S.

7. Serving an Individual in a Foreign Country

8. Serving a Minor or an Incompetent

9. Serving a Corporation, Partnership, or Association

10. Serving the U.S. and its Agencies, Corporations, Officers, and Employees

11. Serving a Foreign State or Local Government

12. Territorial Limits of Effective Service

13. Proving Service

14. Time Limit for Service

15. Asserting Jurisdiction over Property or Assets

J. Pre-Trial Procedures:

1. Injunctions and Restraining Orders (FRCP 65)
   a. Preliminary Injunctions
   b. Temporary Restraining Orders
2. General Rules of Pleading (FRCP 8)
   a. Claim for Relief
   b. Defenses, Admissions, and Denials
   c. Affirmative Defenses
   d. Pleadings must be concise and direct
3. Amended and Supplemental Pleadings (FRCP 15)
   a. Amendments Before Trial
   b. Amendments During and After Trial
   c. Relation Back of Amendments
   d. Supplemental pleadings
4. Representations to the Court and Sanctions (FRCP 11)

K. Joinder

1. Required Joinder of Parties (FRCP 19)
2. Permissive Joinder of Parties (FRCP 20)
3. Joinder of Claims (FRCP 18)

L. Pleadings and Pre-Trial Motions

1. Normal pleadings include:
   a. The Complaint
      1.) This is the plaintiff's statement of his cause of action.
      2.) A complaint starts a lawsuit and serves as notice to the defendant.

      a.) Once a complaint is filed and the defendant does not answer, there is a default judgment entered in favor of the plaintiff.

b. Pre-Answer Motions

1.) The demurrer:

Filed by the defendant before filing an answer if he or she feels that there is no basis for the complaint.

c. The Answer

1.) This document is filed by the defendant and either:

      a.) Admits the allegations made in the complaint or

      b.) Denies them and sets forth any defense the defendant might have.

d. Counterclaims, Cross-claims, and Third-party Claims:

1.) Counterclaims are made by the defendant against the plaintiff arising out of the circumstances of the complaint.

2.) Crossclaims are co-party claims, i.e., brought by a defendant in a lawsuit on a co-defendant.

3.) Third-party claims are also called impleader in which a claim is filed against a third-party not involved in the original lawsuit. Most commonly used with insurance cases.

2. Dismissal/Judgment before Trial
   a. Motion for Judgment on the Pleadings
      1.) Made by either party on the basis that no answer has been filed or that the pleadings show no material issues of fact to be resolved.
   b. Motion for Summary Judgment (FRCP 56)
      1.) Made by either party and is granted if there is no genuine issue of material fact.
   c. Motion to Dismiss Petition for Review or Complaint
      1.) May be filed in lieu of an Answer to the Complaint within the time limit set forth for the Answer.
   d. Motion to Dismiss for lack of jurisdiction
      1.) Made by either party at any time.

M. Discovery:

The process of gathering evidence about the case.

1. Types of Discovery Devices
   a. Interrogatories:
      Written questions sent by one party to another to be answered in writing and under oath.
   b. Depositions:
      A proceeding in which a witness or party is asked questions to be answered under oath before a court reporter.

c. Request for Admission:
   A request to a party to admit certain facts.

d. Request for Production of Documents:
   A request between parties to produce certain defined documents.

e. Request for Physical or Mental Examination:
   Court may order when a party's Physical or mental condition is in controversy.

f. Request for Inspection:
   Issued by the court request an appearance of a witness in court.

g. Subpoena/Subpoena *duces tecum:*
   Issued by the court to request certain documents be turned over to the court by a witness or for the witness to bring them to a deposition.

2. Pre-Trial Hearing:
   A meeting prior to the trial attended by the parties and attorneys in a lawsuit, meant to resolve some of the legal issues before the trial begins.

N. The Trial

1. Right to Trial by Jury
   a. *Voir Dire* (Jury selection)

2. The Case
   a. Opening Statements
   b. Evidence

    c. Closing Statements

    d. Jury Instructions

    e. Motion for a New Trial

    f. Motion for Judgment NOV (Judgment Notwithstanding the Verdict)

    g. Motion for a Directed Verdict:

        1.) Motion for Judgment as a Matter of Law (JMOL) is made by the defendant at the end of the plaintiff's case or at the end of all the evidence.

        2.) Claims that the evidence is insufficient to reasonably support the plaintiff's case.

        3.) In a jury trial, the judge directs the jury to return a particular verdict after finding no reasonable jury could reach any other decision.

3. Appeal:

Application to a higher court for a reversal of the decision of a lower court, usually made by the party who lost the case.

    a. Determination by the court will be:

        1.) *Remanded* (sent back to the trial court);

        2.) *Reversed* (the appellate court overturns the decision of the trial court); or

        3.) *Affirmed* (the decision of the trail court stands the same).

O. Verdict and Judgments

1. Judicial Findings and Conclusions (FRCP 52)

2. Former Adjudication

a. Claim Preclusion (*Res Judicata*):
   A matter that has been adjudicated by a competent court may not be pursued further by the same parties.
b. Issue Preclusion (Collateral Estoppel):
   A common law doctrine that prevents a person from relitigating an issue.

Extra Credit:

As you can see, I added important court cases as well as references to specific Federal Rules of Civil Procedure (FRCP) into my general outline for this course; however, I included landmark cases from Torts and Contracts into my specific outline, rather than the brief one. The reason I did it this way is because civil procedure relies heavily on case law as well as the FRCP for the specific rules you will be learning, especially concerning jurisdiction. It is good to memorize some of these cases and rules if possible for your final exam in this class.

Criminal Law Outline

As you can see, all of my outlines are structured differently, depending on the specific course and what the professor of each class was emphasizing. For Criminal Law, I chose to organize my general outline in such a way that I could immediately spot the different crimes and defenses. Again, for my specific outline, I wrote out all the differing common law versus model penal code rules, as well as important cases regarding these various areas of Criminal Law. Furthermore, there are many rules and nuances that pertain to each of the headings that I have outlined. I also want to note that although I covered Criminal Law and Criminal Procedure in one chapter in this book, I have split them into two separate outlines, as they are two distinct classes you will take in law school.

I. Definition of a Crime:
A wrong or offense against society.

A. Requirements:
Act + Intent + Result = Crime − Defenses

B. Two Essential Elements of Criminal Liability

1. *Actus Reus:*

   The performance of an act prohibited by society the act must be voluntary. Thoughts alone are insufficient to establish the *actus reus* element.

2. *Mens Rea:*

   A specific state of mind or intent on the part of the defendant.

a. Common law jurisdictions draw a distinction between specific and general intent crimes, while Model Penal Code (MPC) jurisdictions do not.

   1.) Specific Intent:
      Requires doing an act with the specific intent to cause social harm.

   2.) General Intent:
      All crimes require general intent, which must occur at the same time as the *actus reus*.

C. Model Penal Code (MPC)

1. Set of criminal law principles and guidelines issued in 1962 which attempt to rationalize criminal law in relation to modern society.

2. Even though the MPC is a statutory work, no jurisdiction is required to adhere to it and its guidelines.

II. The Purposes of Criminal Law

A. Punitive:
To punish those who do wrong.

B. Incapacitation:
Imprisonment to protect society from harm.

C. Deterrence:
To deter others from same behavior.

D. Rehabilitation:
Rehabilitate defendant into a "good citizen."

E. Restitution:

1. The court, as part of a sentence in a criminal case, orders a defendant to compensate the victim for losses suffered as a result of the crime.

2. All states have *laws* requiring that convicted defendants pay *restitution* to their victims.

III. The Process of Proof in a Criminal Case

A. General rule:

State has the burden of proving ALL elements of the crime beyond a reasonable doubt.

B. State generally has burden of production and persuasion.

1. Burden of Production:
   Enough evidence to put a fact at issue.

2. Burden of Persuasion:
   To convince the trier of fact.

IV. Classification of Crimes

A. Felonies:

Punishable by death or imprisonment in a federal or state penitentiary for more than one year.

1. Crimes Against the Person
   a. Homicide:
      The act of one human killing another.
      1.) Murder
         a.) Common Law Murder:
            The unlawful killing of a human being with *malice aforethought*.

b.) Statutory First-Degree Murder:
Unlawful premeditated and deliberate
killing.

c.) First Degree Felony Murder:
Death occurs during the commission or
attempted commission of certain violent
felonies as specified by statute, such as
arson, kidnapping, robbery, burglary and
rape.

d.) Second Degree Murder:
Intentional killing *without* premeditation
and deliberation.

2.) Manslaughter

a.) Common Law Voluntary Manslaughter:
The unlawful killing of a person without
malice upon a sudden heat of passion due
to reasonable provocation.

b.) Common Law Involuntary
Manslaughter
Death caused by criminal negligence or
death caused by an unlawful act.

b. Rape & Sexual Assault

1.) Common Law Rape:
Forced sexual intercourse against a
person's will

2.) Modern Definition of Rape:
The crime of forcing another person to
submit to sex acts.

3.) Statutory Rape:

Sexual intercourse with a child under the age of consent.

4.) Modern statutory rape laws protect underage victims, both male and female, and neither consent nor mistake is a defense in most jurisdictions.

c. Assault:

Attempted battery:

Intentional attempt, using violence or force, to injure or harm another person.

d. Battery:

Intentional harmful/offensive touching without consent.

2. Crimes Relating to Property

a. Arson

1.) Common Law:

Malicious burning of the dwelling of another.

2.) Modern statutes:

Purposeful burning of a structure.

b. Burglary

1.) Common Law:

Breaking and entering of the dwelling home of another at nighttime with the intent to commit a felony.

2.) Modern Statutes:

a.) Expanded to include entering any

structure with intent to commit felony or theft offense inside. Some jurisdictions extend burglary to vehicles.

b.) The nighttime element from common law has been eliminated.

c. Larceny

1.) Trespassory taking and carrying away of the personal property of another with the intent to permanently deprive him or her of that property.

2.) Larceny includes finding lost property with the knowledge or means of discovering ownership.

d. Larceny by Trick:
Obtaining possession by fraud.

e. Embezzlement:
Unlawful possession of property obtained lawfully.

1.) Owner gives possession of property based on trust and the defendant fraudulently or unlawfully converts the owner's entrusted property for his or her own use.

f. False Pretenses:
Obtaining title to property by fraud.

1.) Involves sale or trade transactions.

g. Robbery

1.) Larceny + Assault

2.) A crime at common law and defined as the unlawful taking of property from the person of another through the use of threat or force.

3. Inchoate Crimes:

Also known as incomplete crimes.

a. Acts involving the tendency to commit or to indirectly participate in a criminal offense.

b. Examples of inchoate crimes:

1.) Conspiracy:

Agreement between two or more persons to commit a crime at some time in the future.

2.) Attempt:

Overt act coupled with specific intent to commit a crime.

3.) Solicitation:

Encouraging, aiding, abetting, or ordering another person to commit a crime with the intent that the other person commit the crime.

4. Accomplice Liability:

Aiding, abetting, or counseling.

B. Misdemeanors:

All crimes punishable by imprisonment of one year or less, or by fine only.

Examples include public intoxication, vagrancy, prostitution, larceny (petit), disturbing the peace, and assault and battery.

V. *Malum In Se* and *Malum Prohibitum*

A. *Malum in se* (wrong in itself)

1. A crime that is inherently evil.

2. Battery and larceny are *malum in se.*

3. Crimes of moral turpitude are often *malum in se.*

B. *Malum prohibitum:*

1. Crimes that are wrong because the legislature says they are.

2. Examples of *malum prohibitum* crimes:

   a. Traffic violations;

   b. Failure to comply with the Federal Drug Labeling Act.

VI. Double Jeopardy Clause of the Fifth Amendment

A. Once convicted, subsequent prosecutions for the same and other lesser included offenses by the same jurisdiction are prohibited.

1. Exception:

   Multiple convictions for the same conduct by different jurisdictions are allowed and do *not* violate double jeopardy (e.g., state and federal criminal charges for the same conduct).

B. Double jeopardy protection does NOT apply to sentencing.

1. Prior criminal conduct, charged or uncharged, convicted or acquitted, can be used in a subsequent sentencing [*Witte v. U.S.*, 515 U.S. 389 (1995)].

C. Double jeopardy does NOT protect from imposition of both criminal and civil punishment for the same conduct [*Hudson v. U.S.*, 522 U.S. 93 (1997)].

VI. Defenses to Criminal Liability
A. Defenses Against a Crime:
1. Justification:
a. Crimes Against the Person:
1.) Justifiable use of force for self-defense, defense of property, and prevention of a crime.

a.) Nondeadly Force:

A person may use such force as reasonably appears necessary to prevent the imminent use of unlawful force on him or her, short of deadly force.

b.) Deadly Force:

May only be used in *self-defense* when the threat is imminent, response is necessary, and deadly force is proportionate to the threat.

1.] Defense of Property:

Only non-deadly force may be used to defend one's property in most jurisdictions.

2.] A small minority of jurisdictions allow the use of deadly force to defend property.

c.) Duty to Retreat Rule

1.] At common law, one must retreat rather than use deadly force unless at one's home or business (Castle Doctrine).

2.] Some jurisdictions mandate that there is no duty to retreat unless retreat can be made safely.

3.] Some jurisdictions do not require a duty to retreat, even if it can be done safely.

d.) Stand your Ground Jurisdiction (current legal trend):

Many jurisdictions are now abandoning the duty to retreat rule and instead allow individuals to 'stand your ground' even in instances where retreat could be done safely.

b. Defense of Others

1.) Another defense that can be used when a criminal defendant commits a criminal act but believes that he or she was justified in doing so.

2.) *Defense of others, like self-defense,* also recognizes the right to use reasonable force in *defense of others* who are threatened.

c. Necessity:

Otherwise-criminal conduct is justifiable if, as a result of pressure from natural forces, the defendant reasonably believes that his or her conduct was necessary to avoid harm to self or society.

d. Consent:

Consent by the victim can form the basis of a justification defense to criminal conduct.

1.) Most commonly used as a defense to sex crimes such as rape.

2.) This defense can be statutory or common law, depending on the jurisdiction.

3.) Consent to a crime is not a defense to murder, prostitution or drug use.

e. Duress:

Unlawful pressure exerted upon a person to coerce that person to perform an act that he or she ordinarily would not perform.

1.) Except with respect to homicide, a person compelled to commit a crime by an unlawful threat from another person to injure him, her, or a third person, will generally not be held responsible for its commission.

2. Other defenses

a. Mistake of Fact:

Can be a defense if it negates the intent on the part of the defendant to commit the crime.

b. Mistake of Law:

Normally not a defense except:

1.) Entrapment by estoppel.

2.) If statute requires proof of defendant's

knowledge of the law (due process) defense (Lambert principle).

    a.) In Lambert v. California, 355 U.S. 224 (1957), the court held that knowledge or probability of knowledge of a statute is required to convict someone of a notice offense.

  c. Entrapment

B. Criminal Capacity Defenses

1. Infancy
   a. Common law v. statutory age varies in some states.
   b. Common law rules:
      1.) Under age 7, a child is conclusively presumed incapable of knowing wrongfulness of crimes.
      2.) Aged 7 to 14, there is a rebuttable presumption of incapacity.
      3.) Aged over 14 years, a child can form criminal intent.

2. Insanity
   a. There is a presumption of sanity.
   b. Burden is on defendant to come forward with evidence sufficient to raise a reasonable doubt about sanity.

3. Intoxication
   a. Voluntary v. involuntary intoxication

C. Constitutional Defenses

1. Void for Vagueness:
   Reasonable people must necessarily guess as to the meaning of the law.

2. Overbroad:
   A statute gives a state too much power by possibly prohibiting conduct that is protected by the U.S. Constitution.
   a. Usually involves infringements on First Amendment rights.

3. Cruel and Unusual Punishment:
   Under the Eighth Amendment, individuals convicted of a crime have the right to be free of "cruel and unusual" punishment while in jail or prison.

4. Death Penalty:
   Reserved for the most serious murder cases.

5. Equal Protection:
   A criminal statute can be deemed unconstitutional on Fourteenth Amendment grounds if it fails to provide persons within its jurisdiction equal protection under the law.

6. Supremacy Clause:
   Any constitutionally sound federal law trumps a conflicting state law (USC, Article VI, Clause 2).

7. *Ex post facto* Law:
   Laws that retroactively make illegal an act that was

legal when committed, increase the penalties for an infraction after it has been committed, or changes the rules of evidence to make convictions easier.

    a. The Constitution (Article I, Section 10, Clause 1) prohibits the making of *ex post facto* laws.

8. Bill of Attainder:

Prevents punishment without a trial.

Criminal Procedure Outline

I. Sources of Criminal Procedure Law

   A. The *United States Constitution* (USC), specifically the Bill of Rights, is the main source for criminal procedure law.

      1. Pertinent Amendments

         a. Fourth Amendment:
Freedom from unreasonable searches and seizures.

         b. Fifth Amendment:
Freedom from self-incrimination.

         c. Sixth Amendment:

            1.) Right to assistance of counsel; and

            2.) Right to a speedy trial:
Applies directly to federal prosecutions and applies to state prosecutions through the Fourteenth Amendment Due Process Clause.

         d. Eighth Amendment:
Freedom from cruel and unusual punishment.

   B. *Federal Rules of Ciminal Procedure* (FRCP)

   C. Federal Statutes

   D. State Statutes

II. Overview of a Criminal Proceeding

   A. Probable Cause for Arrest

B. Police Station Booking

C. Filing Charges

D. First Appearance

E. Preliminary Hearing

F. Information or Indictment

G. Arraignment

H. Pretrial

I. Motion for Discovery

J. Trial

1. Jury trial

2. Confrontation clause

3. Defendant's right to remain silent and not to testify at trial

4. Presumption of innocence

K. Sentencing

1. Procedural rights

2. Review of a court's decision

3. Re-sentencing after appeal

4. The death penalty

L. Double Jeopardy

M. Post-Conviction Relief:

A general term related to appeals of criminal convictions, which may include release, new trial, modification of sentence, and such other relief as may be proper and just.

1. Appeals

2. Collateral Remedies:

Certain defendants can request collateral relief

to avoid some of the long-term consequences of having a criminal conviction on their record.

3. *Habeas Corpus:*

A writ (court order), which is a judicial mandate, to a prison official ordering that an inmate be brought to the court so it can be determined whether or not that person is imprisoned lawfully and whether or not he should be released from custody.

III. The Fourteenth Amendment and its Incorporation by the States

A. The Fourteenth Amendment provides that no state "may deprive any person of life, liberty, or property, without due process of law."

B. Incorporation of the Fourteenth Amendment extends the Due Process requirements provided under the Bill of Rights to the states.

IV. The Fourth Amendment: The Right Against Unreasonable Search and Seizure

A. Limitations:

Limited to conduct by the government or an agent of the government.

B. What is a search?

1. Old approach:

Trespassory invasion of person or tangible property [*Olmstead v. United States,* 277 U.S. 438 (1928)].

2. Modern approach:

Two-prong test for when a reasonable expectation of privacy is violated [*Katz v. United States*, 389 U.S. 347 (1967)]:

   a. Actual expectation of privacy (subjective).

   b. Expectation must be one that society is prepared to recognize as reasonable (objective).

C. Seizures are Protected by the Fourth Amendment

1. Property

2. Persons

D. Reasonableness

1. Scope

   a. The Fourth Amendment protects against unreasonable searches and seizures.

   b. The standards used to determine reasonableness depend on circumstances.

2. Probable cause:

   Facts and circumstances sufficient for a reasonable person to believe a crime is more likely than not; if so, the proposed arrest or search is justified.

3. Reasonable suspicion:

   Officer must have a reasonable basis for suspicion that a crime is afoot.

4. Special standards for reasonableness (balancing approach).

E. Warrant Requirement of the Fourth Amendment

1. The Fourth Amendment states, "No Warrants shall issue, but upon probable cause," which is required for both search warrants and arrest warrants.

a. Search warrants must be issued by a magistrate or judicial officer.

1.) Affidavit

2.) Place to be searched

3.) Property to be seized

4.) Manner in which search warrant is executed

5.) Unannounced entry

6.) Search of other persons on premises

7.) Plain view

8.) Body searches

b. Arrest warrants:

Generally not required for felony arrest in public place as long as probable cause exists [*U.S. v. Watson*, 423 *U.S.* 411 (1976)].

c. Exception to search warrant

1.) Search incident to arrest

2.) Automobile search incident to arrest

3.) Exigent circumstances

4.) Automobile exception:

Entire car may be searched without a warrant if probable cause exists and exigency created by car's mobility [*Carroll v. United States*, 267 U.S. 132 (1925)].

5.) Inventory searches of cars

6.) Consent searches

7.) Third-party consent

d. Terry stop:

Warrantless brief detention and "Stop and

Frisk." Police may seize person briefly without probable cause so long as there is reasonable suspicion of criminal activity [*Terry v. Ohio*, 392 U.S. 1 (1968)].

   e. Reasonableness of seizures

   1.) Arrest requires probable cause and sometimes requires a warrant.

   2.) Terry seizures require reasonable suspicion.

   f. Ad hoc balancing:
   Permits full search for evidence without warrant so long as search is "reasonable".

   g. Administrative searches:
   Warrant required in most cases.

   h. Border searches:
   Both citizens and non-citizens have no Fourth Amendment rights at a border or its functional equivalent [*Almeida-Sanchez v. United States*, 413 *U.S.* 266 (1973)].

V. Judicial Doctrines

A. Exclusionary Rule:

A law that prohibits the use of illegally obtained evidence in a criminal trial.

1. Applies to Fourth, Fifth, and Sixth Amendment rights violations.

2. Applicable to federal cases [*Weeks v. United States*, 232 U.S. 383 (1914)].

3. Applicable to states [*Mapp v. Ohio*, 367 U.S. 643 (1961)].

B. Fruit of the Poisonous Tree:

No, you can't eat that! This tree is poisonous.

1. This doctrine extends the exclusionary rule to make evidence inadmissible in court if it was derived from evidence that was illegally obtained. As this legal metaphor implies, if the evidential "*tree*" is tainted, so is its "*fruit*".

2. Exceptions to the exclusionary rule
   a. Independent Source Doctrine
   b. Inevitable Discovery Doctrine
   c. Attenuation Doctrine
   d. Limitations on the Exclusionary Rule
      1.) Not applicable to grand juries.
      2.) Not applicable in civil proceedings.

3.) Not applicable in parole revocation hearings.

4.) Not applicable to evidence seized in violation of the "knock and announce" rule when search of a home was otherwise supported by a valid search warrant.

    a.) *"Knock-and-announc*e" is a common law principle, incorporated into the Fourth Amendment, which requires law enforcement officers to *announce* their presence and provide residents with an opportunity to open the door prior to a search.

e. Good-faith exception:
The exclusionary rule does not apply when police act in "good faith reliance" on an existing statutory law or ordinance.

f. Impeaching testimony defendant exception.

g. Physical evidence gained from Miranda violations exception.

VI. The Fifth Amendment: Confessions
A. Due Process

1. Involuntary Confessions:
These types of confessions violate due process and cannot be used for any purpose [*Spano v. New York*, 360 U.S. 315 (1959)].

2. Voluntary Confessions:
Totality of the circumstances taken into account.

3. *Miranda* Rights:

Protection based on the Fifth Amendment right not to incriminate oneself.

a. The *Miranda* warnings originated in a U.S. Supreme Court ruling, *Miranda v. Arizona*, 384 U.S. 436 (1966), which set forth the following warnings and accompanying rights:

1.) Right to remain silent.

2.) Anything said can be used against suspect in court.

3.) Right to presence of an attorney.

4.) Attorney will be provided without cost if suspect cannot afford one.

B. *Miranda* **rights are triggered by custody and interrogation.**

1. Custodial interrogations require *Miranda* warnings to be given.

2. Custody:

Arrest, or functional equivalent of arrest, defines custody for *Miranda* purposes.

a. Objective test used to determine custody is whether a reasonable person in the suspect's position, considering the circumstances surrounding the interrogation, would believe he or she is in custody.

3. Interrogation:

a. Questioning in the form of an officer asking the suspect direct questions; or

b. Comments or actions by the officer that the officer should know are likely to produce an incriminating reply.

c. Volunteered statements are not protected by Miranda.

4. Invocation of rights:

Once a suspect declares the right to counsel, police may not question him or her again without counsel present.

5. Limitations:

Miranda requirements do not apply to witnesses testifying before a grand jury.

6. Effect of Miranda violation

a. Evidence obtained in violation of Miranda is inadmissible at trial.

b. Physical evidence found as a result of a suspect's un-Mirandized but voluntary statement is admissible.

c. If the defendant takes the stand at trial, the prosecution can use a confession obtained in violation of Miranda to impeach his or her testimony.

VII. The Sixth Amendment: Right to Counsel

A. The Sixth Amendment provides a defendant counsel at felony or misdemeanor trials where actual jail time is imposed [*Gideon v. Wainwright*, 372 U.S. 335 (1963)].

1. The court, in *Gideon v. Wainright*, made the Sixth

Amendment right applicable to the states by the Fourteenth Amendment.

2. Stages where the right to counsel applies
   a. Post-charge physical line ups
   b. Post-indictment interrogation (whether custodial or not) by known and/or undercover government agents.
   c. Arraignment
   d. Misdemeanor trials when imprisonment is imposed
   e. Juvenile delinquency proceedings in which institutional commitment is a possibility
   f. Felony trials
   g. Guilty pleas and sentencing
   h. Appeals as a matter of right
   i. Right to paid counsel of choice, including *pro hac vice:*
      An attorney who doesn't live, work or conduct regular business in the state can petition the court to represent his or her client under this title. It is a Latin term that means "for this occasion".

3. Stages at which right to counsel does not apply
   a. Photo IDs
   b. Taking of handwriting, fingerprints, voice exemplars
   c. Discretionary appeals
   d. Post-conviction proceedings

4. The Sixth Amendment right to counsel guarantees effective assistance of counsel [*Strickland v. Washington*, 466 U.S. 668 (1984)].

VIII. The Eighth Amendment: Cruel and Unusual Punishment

A. The *Eighth Amendment* to the United States Constitution states: "Excessive bail shall not be required, nor excessive fines imposed, nor *cruel and unusual punishments* inflicted."

1. Example: The court held, in *Miller v. Alabama*, 567 U.S. 460 (2012), that a mandatory life sentence without parole should not apply to juveniles convicted of murder.

2. This clause measures a particular punishment against society's prohibition against inhuman treatment, and prevents the government from imposing a penalty that is far too severe for the crime committed.

Extra Credit:

I included in this general outline several key landmark cases for some of the principles we learned; however, there were also many more cases that illustrated important facets of criminal procedure, and I put those in my more detailed outline. Filling out my general outlines with all the specific rules and case examples helped me to remember them on the final exam.

In addition, I wanted to point out how movies and television shows commonly portray police officers arresting and handcuffing suspects, reading them their *Miranda* rights, and questioning them. But *Miranda* comes into play in more scenarios than just this one, such as custody and interrogation as shown in my outline above.

There are many criminal procedure topics which are covered on the MBE. To refresh your memory, the Multistate Bar Examination (**MBE**) is a six-hour, 200-question multiple-choice examination developed by the National Conference of Bar Examiners. The MBE is administered by user jurisdictions as part of the bar examination on the last Wednesday in February and the last Wednesday in July of each year. Here is a list of some of the criminal procedure/evidence MBE topics covered on previous bar exams.

1. Arrest, search and seizure
2. Confessions and privilege against self-incrimination
3. Lineups and other forms of identification
4. Right to counsel
5. Fair trail and guilty pleas
6. Double jeopardy
7. Cruel and unusual punishment
8. Burdens of proof and persuasion
9. Appeal and error
10. Evidence

Real Property Outline

I. Classification of Property

A. Personal property:

Movable property, including belongings exclusive of land and buildings.

B. Real property:

Refers to the land, including structures and minerals.

II. Ownership Interests in Real Property: Estates in Land

A. Rights of ownership in real property are called "estates."

B. Present Possessory Estates: Freehold Estates

1. Fee Simple Absolute
   a. Creation
      1.) "To A," "To A and his heirs," or "To A in fee simple"
   b. Duration
      1.) Has the potential to last forever
   c. Alienability:
      Ability to convey or transfer property to another.
      1.) Freely alienable
2. Defeasible Fees
   a. Fee Simple Determinable
      1.) Creation
         a.) "To A and his heirs, *so long as* they use the and for specific purposes only"

2.) Duration

    a.) Potentially infinite duration, as long as the condition is not violated.

    b.) The grantor retains a future interest called a "possibility of reverter."

3.) Alienability

    a.) Freely alienable

b. Fee Simple Subject to a Condition Subsequent

1.) Creation

    a.) "To A and his heirs, but if the land is used for other than specified purposes, Grantee or his heirs shall have the right to enter and declare the estate forfeited."

2.) Duration

    a.) The grantor keeps possession until the grantor enters and terminates the estate.

3.) Alienability

    a.) The estate is feely alienable, subject to the condition.

c. Fee Simple Subject to an Executory Interest Similar to an ordinary fee simple determinable or one subject to a condition subsequent except that if the condition is broken the estate goes to a third party and not the grantor.

3. Fee Tail

a. Creation

1.) "To A and the heirs of A's body" (to keep ownership of land within the family)

    b. Duration

        1.) At common law, the grantee received an estate for his life, which passed to his first heir at his death.

    c. Alienability

        1.) At common law, the grantee could not transfer an interest in the estate that exceeded his lifetime.

        2.) Modern view in most states has been to abolish the fee tail or greatly modify its effect.

4. Life Estate

    a. Creation

        1.) "To A for life."

    b. Duration

        1.) Grantee's lifetime

    c. Alienability

        1.) The grantee is free to make transfers during his life, but possession of the land by the third party terminates at the death of the original grantee.

        2.) Common law: Presumption of life estate unless words or limitation and inheritance to the contrary.

        3.) Modern trend: Courts favor fee simple absolute

C. Future Interests:

Estates which become possessory in the future.

1. A transferor who conveys or wills his property to another can retain part of his interest.

2. Three types of future interests a transferor can retain:
   a. Reversion
   b. Possibility of reverter
   c. Right of entry

3. Transferred future interests
   a. A grantor may also limit future interest in a transferee.
   b. Two types of future interests that a transferee can have:
      1.) Remainders
         a.) Vested and contingent remainders
      2.) Executory interests
         a.) Springing executory interest
         b.) Shifting executory interest

4. The rule against perpetuities:
   Prohibits a grant of an estate unless the interest must vest, if at all, no later than twenty-one years after the death of some person alive when the interest is created.
   a. Interests subject to the rule:
      1.) Springing and shifting executory interests;
      2.) Contingent remainders; and
      3.) Vested remainders subject to open
   b. Interests that are NOT subject to the rule:
      1.) Reversions;

      2.) Rights of entry;

      3.) Possibilities of reverter; and

      4.) Vested remainders

D. Rule against Restraints on Alienation

  1. Conditions or covenants in grants that restrain the grantee's right to transfer his or her interest are void under certain circumstances.

  2. Three types of restrictions placed on the alienation of land that courts will invalidate

    a. Disability restrictions

    b. Forfeiture restrictions

    c. Promissory restrictions

E. Concurrent Estates:

Ownership of real property by two or more persons.

  1. Joint tenancy

    a. Right of survivorship

      1.) Property automatically passes to the survivor when one of the original owners dies. Real estate, bank accounts, vehicles, and investments can all pass this way.

      2.) No probate is necessary to transfer ownership of the property.

      3.) Can apply to property held in joint tenancy, tenancy by the entirety, or community property with the right of survivorship.

    b. Four unities (a joint tenancy agreement's legal requirements) required:

      1.) Unity of interest

        2.) Unity of possession

        3.) Unity of time

        4.) Unity of title

   c. Involuntary severance (creditor's lien)

        1.) No severance for a judicial sale

   d. Voluntary partition

        1.) Mortgage

        2.) Lease

2. Tenant by the entirety:

   a. A small number of states recognize this form of joint tenancy that can only be created between husband and wife.

        1.) Must be married at the time they acquire the property and must remain married in order for the tenancy by the entirety to be valid.

        2.) Deed must refer to the party's marital relationship.

   b. Unities required

        1.) Time

        2.) Title

        3.) Interest

        4.) Possession

   c. "By the whole" means there's no right of partition.

   d. Severance

        1.) Right of survivorship, so that upon the death of one, the survivor is entitled to the decedent's share.

2.) Divorce

    a.) The couple must divorce, obtain an annulment, or agree to amend the title to the property to extinguish a tenancy by the entirety.

3.) Execution proceedings in favor of joint creditor

e. Immune from individual creditors, but federal tax claim may attach to property.

3. Tenant in common:

All tenants in common hold an individual, undivided ownership interest in the property.

a. No right of survivorship; interest passes to the heirs of deceased tenant or the persons named in his or her will.

b. Ownership by part, but right to possess entire property unless restricted by agreement.

c. Freely alienable (an interest in property is alienable if it may be conveyed by one individual to another).

d. Subject to creditor claims.

4. Community property:

The laws in community property *states* vary in their specific details, but community property means that all assets purchased or acquired by a couple during their marriage are owned equally by both of them, regardless of how the asset is titled. Gifts and inheritances are an exception.

III. Landlord and Tenant: Non-Freehold Estates

A. These are possessory interests in real property held for a specific period of time.

B. They are often called leasehold estates.

C. Owner holds future interest in the non-freehold estate and is referred to as landlord.

D. Holder of current interest in the non-freehold estate is usually referred to as tenant.

E. Types of Non-Freehold Estates

    1. Tenancy for years

        a. For specific period of time.

        b. Termination at end of period does not require notice as tenant is aware of the termination date from the outset.

    2. Periodic tenancy:

       A tenancy that continues for successive periods until tenant gives notice he or she wants to end the tenancy.

        a. Automatic renewal: Month to month, or year to year.

        b. Tenancy can be created expressly or implied.

        c. Termination by notification equal to the length of period of tenancy.

    3. Tenancy at will

        a. No fixed duration.

        b. Can be terminated by landlord or tenant at any time.

        c. Exists without a written contract or lease.

4. Tenancy at sufferance
   a. A wrongful "hold-over" tenancy after lease has expired but before landlord has demanded the tenant quit or vacate.
   b. Landlord has option to evict tenant or hold tenant to another term.

F. **Landlord's Rights and Duties**
   1. Common Law: No liability for subsequent arising conditions and no duty to maintain property.
   2. Modern Law: Assumption of repairs (not universal), duty to disclose latent defects, and duty not to interfere with tenant's quiet enjoyment.

G. **Tenant's Rights and Duties**
   1. Tenant has duty to pay rent and duty to maintain property in reasonably good repair.
   2. Tenant is entitled to possession and quiet enjoyment of property without interference by landlord.
   3. Tenant is entitled to implied warranty of habitability:
      a. Warranty implied by law in all residential leases that the premises are fit and habitable and will remain so throughout the duration of the lease.
      b. The warranty conditions a tenant's duty to pay rent on the landlord's duty to maintain a habitable living space.
      c. Remedies for breach of implied warranty of habitability

1.) Vacate the premises;

2.) Retain premises but withhold rent;

3.) Repair and deduct cost from rent; or

4.) Take landlord to court.

H. Illegal Evictions

1. Constructive Eviction:

   Provoked by landlord's substantial interference with tenant's enjoyment of the property, such as cutting off power, water, or gas.

   a. Court may force landlord to uphold provisions of lease agreement.

   b. Tenant may be able to recover damages through lawsuit.

2. Retaliatory Eviction:

   A landlord's action is retaliatory when the landlord punishes the tenant for the tenant's exercise of a legal right, such as complaining of housing code violations, etc.

I. Assignments and Subleases:

Assuming there is no provision in a lease that prohibits transfers, a tenant may freely transfer their leasehold interest in whole or in part.

A. Assignment

1. A lessee transfers the entire remaining estate

B. Sublease

1. A lessee retains any part of a leased estate

IV. Rights of Possessor of Land

A. Lateral Support:

Adjoining lands are side-by-side.

Entitles a landowner to the right of not having their neighbor excavate land that might cause damage to surrounding property.

B. Subjacent Support:

Adjoining lands are above and below.

1. The right of the surface land to be supported by the land beneath it against collapsing.
2. Includes support from the minerals, soil, and even water directly under the surface of the owner's property.

C. Water Rights:

1. Riparian rights are certain rights of all landowners whose properties abut a running body of water, such as a lake, river, or stream.

   a. Rights can include such things as:

      1.) The right to access for swimming, boating and fishing;

      2.) The right to erect structures such as docks, piers, and boat lifts;

      3.) The right to use the water for domestic purposes;

V. Transfer of Ownership of Real Property

A. Ways in which ownership of real property can be conveyed (conveyancing is the act of transferring property to a new owner).

1. Deed (document that transfers ownership of real estate)
   a. Identifies the buyer (grantee) and seller (grantor)
   b. Provides a legal description of the property
   c. Must be signed by the person transferring the property
   d. Types of deeds
      1.) Warranty deed is a type of deed where the grantor guarantees that he or she holds clear title to a piece of real estate and has a right to sell it to the grantee.
         a.) General warranty deed covers defects arising before and during grantor's occupancy.
         b.) Special warranty deed covers defects arising only during grantor's occupancy.
      2.) Quitclaim deed
         a.) Grantor offers the grantee no warranty as to the status of the property title.
         b.) The grantee is entitled only to whatever interest the grantor actually possesses at the time the transfer occurs.

B. Servitude:

The right a person has over the immovable property of another person.
1. A device that ties rights and obligations to ownership or possession of land so that they run

with the land to successive owners and occupiers.

2. Types of servitude

    a. Covenants contained in warranty deeds (grantor warrants title)

        1.) Covenants are conditions tied to the ownership or use of the land.

            a.) Present covenants do not run with the land. "Running with the land" refers to the rights and covenants in a real estate deed that remain with the land, regardless of ownership.

            b.) Future covenants run with the land where privity of estate exists between the original grantor and the present grantee (privity of estate is a mutual or successive relationship to the same right in property)

    b. Easements:

    Grant of interest in land; a limited right to use another person's land for a stated purpose.

        1.) Creation by:

            a.) Express Grant:

            In writing with formalities of deed and duration generally limited for purpose and use.

                1.] Easement appurtenant (e.g., access road)

                    i.] Passes automatically with possession of dominant tenement ii] Restricted to access to attached property

2.] Easement in gross (e.g., pipeline, utility)

  i.] Right of special use independent of ownership.

  ii.] Easement is not appurtenant to other land.

  iii.] Common Law: Personal to original holder and non-inheritable.

  iv.] Modern statutes: Commercial purposes freely transferable.

b.) Implication (Implied Easements): Grant of the right of use is implied and not formally written or deeded.

1.] Land is landlocked, and the necessity of the easement is based on public policy or intention of parties to create an easement.

c.) Necessity: When one parcel of land is sold, depriving the other parcel of access to a public road or utility.

d. Prescription

1.] Continuous and uninterrupted use. Periodic or seasonal use is sufficient.

2.] 20 years by statute of limitation.

3.] Adverse use of another's land ends
when use is interrupted by owner.

i.] New prescriptive period starts
after interruption.

4.] Visible and notorious or with
knowledge and acquiescence

5.] Majority of jurisdictions recognize
public easements, especially
customary right to use beaches.

2.) Types of Easements

a.) Dominant tenement (right of use for
special purposes)

b.) Servient tenement (owner retains
possession subject to limitation of right
of use by another.)

3.) Termination of Easements

a.) Release in writing

b.) Merger (owner purchases underlying
estate)

c.) Estoppel

1.] May apply if a holder of the easement
right engages in conduct that
results in the owner of the servient
estate reasonably believing that the
easement has been abandoned.

2.] Owner must act to his or her
detriment based upon that belief.

d.) Abandonment (when the easement

holder takes affirmative action to permanently desert the easement)

    1.] Non-use of the easement alone does not qualify as abandonment

e.) Ending by necessity (no further need for the easement)

f.). Ends when condition occurs

    1.] Destruction of servient tenement by natural causes or by owner's interference

    2.] By alteration of dominant tenement, making the particular purpose originally granted no longer possible to achieve

3.) Profits

a.) Profits give someone the right to enter and remove natural resources (e.g., sand timber, gravel) from the land of another.

b.) Exists for a determinate time.

c.) Subject to statute of frauds.

d.) Restrictions on public land for natural gas.

4.) Equitable Servitude:

An agreement or contract between two or more parties that limits their use of property.

a) Benefits and burdens the original parties to the agreement as well as their predecessors (e.g., a promise to maintain a property as an open park).

b.) Restriction on the use of land and
the remedy is injunction or specific
performance.

C. Mortgages

1. Mortgagee: Creditor/Lender

2. Mortgagor: Debtor/Borrower

3. Conveyance

    a. Must be recorded to give notice to subsequent
purchaser.

4. Mortgage Alternatives

    a. Absolute deed

    b. Installment land contract

    c. Deed of trust

    d. Sale-leaseback

5. Equity of Redemption

6. Foreclosure

D. Licenses:

Permission to enter of use the property of another.

1. Revocable Privilege:

A grant of consent to use another's property that
can be revoked by the licensor at any time with or
without cause.

E. Title Search

1. Marketable Title

    a. Good record title represents unencumbered fee
simple property.

    b. Defects in title rendering it unmarketable may
include:

1.) Improper prior instrument;

2.) A private encumbrance (e.g., mortgage, easement); or

3.) Violation of a zoning ordinance.

2. Quiet Title Act

    a. An action to quiet title is a lawsuit brought in a court having jurisdiction over property disputes, in order to establish a party's title to real property or personal property.

VI. Adverse Possession:

Doctrine under which a person in possession of land owned by someone else may acquire valid title to it as long as certain common law requirements are met, and the adverse possessor is in possession for a sufficient period of time as defined by a statute of limitations.

A. Common Law Requirements

1. Continuous
2. Hostile
3. Open and Notorious
4. Actual
5. Exclusive

B. Statute of Limitations:

A typical statute requires possession for seven years, if under color of title, or twenty years if not.

1. "Color of title" refers to a claim based on a land right, land warrant, land scrip, or an irregular chain of title.

2. The threshold varies by jurisdiction.

VII. Land-Use Control

A. Zoning:

The most common form of land-use regulation.

1. Zoning categories vary among communities
2. Zoning regulations and restrictions are used by municipalities to control and direct the development of property within their border.

B. Eminent Domain:

The right of a government or its agent to confiscate private property for public use, with payment of just compensation.

1. Procedure to "effect" a taking
2. Public use requirement

C. Regulatory Takings

1. Government regulation will frequently limit a property owner's use of his or her land.
2. Case-by-case approach based on the particular circumstances of the cases.

D. Inverse Condemnation

Occurs where a landowner claims that a government action has devalued a private property interest so that compensation should be owed.

Extra Credit:

As we discussed earlier in the book, the current trend in law school is toward consolidation, and some law schools are compressing all the intricacies of property law into one semester. There is a lot of information to learn and understand, and I hope that this general outline overview will make it easier for you. The four topics which are *universally* covered in a property law class, according to the Task Force on Real Property Law School Curricula, are **adverse possession, concurrent ownership, servitudes** (including both easements and covenants running with the land), and **estates** (including future interests).

I would also like to point out how interrelated all your first year core subjects are. For example, we learned about the **statute of frauds** (which applies to land contracts, sale of goods in excess of $500, contracts lasting more than one year, contracts not to be performed during the lifetime of the promiser, and contracts to be responsible for someone else's debt) in my Contracts class, and it came up again in my Real Property class.

Under the statute of frauds, contracts for the sale of an interest in land must be written down and signed by both parties. One exception is if a buyer has paid part of the purchase price and has taken possession of the property or made improvements to it as a result of an oral contract. Another exception is part performance of a real estate agreement. For example, a seller performs his side of the contract by conveying good title to the buyer. Can he recover the purchase price from the buyer even though the contract was oral? The answer is yes. Although the contract was oral and unenforceable under the statute of frauds, part performance and the conveyance of title made the contract enforceable.

Lastly, my Real Property class, as opposed to my Civil and Criminal Procedure classes, relied heavily on common law doctrines. Thus, I did not cite a lot of cases in my general outline.

We still read cases to ascertain the rules of law, but they were not as influential as in other first year classes in terms of studying for my final exams. Instead, the cases were included in our textbook to explore the development of basic principles of property law, such as cases on how property rights are acquired or the content of property rights.

Let's now move onto my sixth outline which was for Evidence.

Evidence Outline
Based on *Federal Rules of Evidence* [FRE]

I. Judicial Notice [FRE 201]:
Acceptance of a fact as true without the necessity of formal proof.

A. Legislative Facts:
Those relevant to legal reasoning and the lawmaking process.
1. Includes statutory law and judicial decisions.

B. Adjudicative Facts:
The facts of a particular case.

C. Mandatory Judicial Notice:
Facts that are so universally known that they cannot reasonably be disputed.
1. When requested by a party [FRE 201 (d)].

D. Permissive Judicial Notice:
Facts that are not reasonably subject to dispute and are capable of accurate determination from undisputable sources, such as encyclopedias (e.g., time of sunrise on a particular date).
1. On its own, the court may take judicial notice of certain matters [FRE 201 (c)].

E. Effect of Judicial Notice
1. Civil Case: It is binding on a jury to accept any fact judicially noticed as conclusively proved.
2. Criminal Case: The jury is instructed that it may, but is not required to, accept any fact judicially noticed as conclusively proved [FRE 201 (g)].

II. Judicial Rulings
A. Rulings on Evidence [FRE 103]
1. Erroneous only if substantial right of party is affected and the nature of the error was called to the attention of the judge.

B. Preliminary Questions [FRE 104]
1. The court determines questions regarding whether:
   a. a witness is qualified;
   b. a privilege exits; or
   c. the evidence is admissible.

III. Burdens of Proof [FRE 301]
A. Burden of Production:
Burden is on the party who asserts a fact to provide evidence to show that fact exists. This burden may shift once a party has satisfied burden of "going forward with the evidence."

B. Burden of Persuasion:
Burden is on the plaintiff to prove the allegations in the complaint and on the defendant to prove all affirmative defenses; these burdens do not shift.

IV. Kinds of Proof
A. Direct evidence proves a proposition directly.
B. Circumstantial evidence tends to prove an issue indirectly through inference.

V. Relevance

A. Tests for Relevance [FRE 401]

1. Does evidence tend to prove or disprove a fact of consequence?
2. Is the fact of consequence in determining action?

B. Limits on Otherwise Relevant Evidence [FRE 402]

1. All relevant evidence is admissible except as excluded by:
   - a.) The United States Constitution
   - b.) A federal statute
   - c.) Other rules prescribed by the Supreme Court

C. Exclusion of Evidence [FRE 403]

1. The court has discretion to exclude relevant evidence when:
   - a.) Its probative value is substantially outweighed by the danger of unfair prejudice;
   - b.) Confusion of the issues;
   - c.) Misleading the jury; or
   - d.) By considerations of undue delay, waste of time, or needless presentation of cumulative evidence.

D. Determining Relevancy

1. Most relevancy problems involve circumstantial evidence.
2. In determining relevancy, evidence must be presented in:
   - a. Proper form (e.g., question properly phrased); and

b. After laying a proper foundation (e.g., competency of witnesses, reliability of scientific tests).

E. Types of Evidence

1. Character in Civil Cases

   a. FRE Rule 404 makes character evidence inadmissible in most circumstances, but admissible under several exceptions:

      1.) When character is an ultimate fact in a dispute;

      2.) Negligent entrustment (the act of leaving an object, such as an automobile or firearm, with another whom the lender knows or should know could use the object to harm others due to such factors as youth or inexperience); or

      3.) Evidence of either reputation in the community or specific acts to show this character trait, and which is indicative of credibility.

2. Character in Criminal Cases [FRE 404]

   a. Generally, bad character is inadmissible to prove defendant is more likely to have committed crime.

   b. Accused may always introduce evidence of good character that tend to show he or she did not commit the crime.

   c. Victim's character in criminal case [FRE 404(a)(2)]:

1.) Admissible in homicide cases.

2.) Inadmissible in rape cases except:

    a.) Victim's sexual behavior may be admissible to prove someone else is source of semen, injury, or physical evidence.

d. Other bad acts [FRE 404(b)]

    1.) Admissible to prove another element of present crime but not to show defendant had criminal propensity.

e. Habit [FRE 406]

    1.) Habit or routine business practice is admissible to prove that the conduct of a person or organization on a specific occasion conformed to the habit or routine.

f. Pleas and Related Statements [FRE 410]

    1.) Withdrawn guilty pleas, pleas of *nolo contendere*, and offers to plead guilty or evidence of statements to prosecute in making such pleas are inadmissible in any proceeding, with some noted exceptions.

g. Rape [FRE 412]:

    1.) Evidence of a victim's past sexual behavior or sexual predisposition is inadmissible in any civil or criminal proceeding, with a few noted exceptions.

h. Documents:

Includes handwriting, voice (telephone),

photographs, x-rays, and ancient documents.

   1.) Best Evidence Rule (FRE 1002)

      a.) Also known as original document rule.

      b.) Applies when a party wants to admit as evidence the contents of a document at trial, but the original is unavailable.

VI. Witnesses

A. Presumption of Competency [FRE 601]

B. Opinion Testimony:

1. Lay witnesses are generally inadmissible [FRE 701].

2. Expert witnesses are generally admissible [FRE 702].

C. Scope of Cross-examination:

Cross-examination should not go beyond the subject matter of the direct examination and matters affecting the witness's credibility. The court may allow inquiry into additional matters as if on direct examination. [FRE 611 (b)]

D. Privileges [FRE 501]:

State and common law principles based on societal desires to encourage particular relationships:

1. Attorney-client;

2. Social worker-client;

3. Physician-patient;

4. Clergy and accountant privileges; and

5. Husband-wife.

E. Leading Questions [FRE 611(c)]:

1. On cross-examination, witness cannot refuse to answer.

2. On direct examination, generally, not allowed *except* when:

   a. Establishing preliminary facts;

   b. Aiding a witness with memory loss;

   c. Questioning hostile witnesses, child witnesses, adult witnesses with communications problems, or timid witnesses; or

   d. Developing testimony as necessary.

VII. Hearsay

Statement made out of court by declarant to prove truth of matter asserted is inadmissible [801(c)]. A statement may be an oral or written assertion or nonverbal conduct intended as an assertion.

A. Statements that are not hearsay [801(d)]

1. Prior inconsistent statement made under oath at a prior proceeding or deposition;

2. Prior consistent statement, whether under oath or not, offered to rebut an express or implied charge of recent fabrication, improper influence or motive on the part of a witness;

3. Prior statement of identification of a person after perceiving him (e.g., lineups, photo IDs);

4. Admission by party opponent:
   An out of court statement or conduct by a party

to the present litigation that is used against him or her.

a. Judicial Admissions

  1.) Civil cases: A party is bound by statements in pleadings;

  2.) Prior criminal case pleadings:

    a.) No contest or *nolo contendere* plea cannot be used as an admission because it does not admit guilt.

    b.) Guilty plea can be introduced as an admission in a subsequent civil or criminal proceeding which involves the same act.

    c.) Adoptive admissions: Generally, where the defendant, knowing the content of an accusation against him, adopts the truth of the accusation by his words or conduct.

    d.) Vicarious admissions made by another may be imputed to party based on certain relationships (includes statements made by conspirators).

B. Hearsay Exceptions [FRE 804]

1. A declarant is considered unavailable as a witness if:

a. Declarant is exempt due to privilege;

b. Declarant refuses to testify despite a court order to do so;

   c. Declarant lacks memory of subject matter or statement;

   d. Declarant is physically unavailable due to:

      1.) Death

      2.) Mental or physical illness

   e. Declarant cannot be subpoenaed (e.g., out of the country)

      1.) Exceptions:

         a.) Former testimony [FRE 804(b)(1)]

         b.) Dying declarations [FRE 804(b)(2)]

         c.) Statements against interest [FRE 804(b)(3)]

         d.) Statements of personal or family history [FRE 804(b)(4)]

         e.) Forfeiture of right to object where party procures unavailability of declarant [FRE 804(b)(6)]

         f.) Residual exception [FRE 807]

2. Where declarant need not be unavailable because guarantees of trustworthiness are inherent:

   a. Present sense impression [FRE 803(1)]

   b. Excited utterance [FRE 803(2)]

   c. Then-existing mental, emotional or physical condition [FRE 803(3)]

   d. Statement for purposes of medical diagnosis or treatment [FRE 803(4)]

   e. Recorded recollections [FRE 803(5)]

      1.) If admitted, the record may be read into

evidence but may be received as an exhibit only if offered by an adverse party.

f. Business records exception [FRE 803(6)]

g. Absence of entry in business records [FRE 803(7)]

h. Public records & reports [FRE 803(8)]

VIII. Constitutional Issues in Criminal Law: Confrontation Clause of the Sixth Amendment

A. **The Sixth Amendment to the U.S. Constitution sets out many rights for defendants during a criminal prosecution, including the right of the accused to confront their accusers.**

1. The Fourteenth Amendment has made the Sixth Amendment's right to confrontation applicable to state court as well as federal court.

B. **Admitting hearsay evidence may violate Confrontation Clause**

1. Prior testimonial evidence is inadmissible against criminal defendant unless:

a. Declarant is unavailable; or

b. Defendant had opportunity to cross-examine hearsay declarant (*Crawford v. Washington*, 541 U.S. 36 (2004)).

Extra credit:

As you can see from the numerous general headings listed above in the Evidence outline, there are many *specific* rules and nuances a law student needs to know about in relation to each particular area of the law. For instance, under the topic of Rape [FRE 412], I listed the general rule that evidence of a victim's past sexual behavior or sexual predisposition is inadmissible in any civil or criminal proceeding, with some noted exceptions. In my own more detailed outline, I listed all those exceptions.

This outline, like all the others in this book, is meant to give you a handle on the many topics covered during your first year law classes, but it is up to you to fill in the details from the information you will learn from class discussions.

Also, I have noted in my outlines any updates to the law. For instance, the *Crawford* case, listed in the section about constitutional issues in criminal law, recedes from *Ohio v. Roberts*, 448 U.S. 56 (1980), a United States Supreme Court decision dealing with the Confrontation Clause of the Sixth Amendment, which is what I studied in law school. In *Ohio*, the court held that a statement made to a third person is admissible if it contained indicia of reliability. Although *Crawford* is a new procedural rule, it does not apply retroactively.

Lastly, on the bar examination, you may encounter an essay which combines the subjects of Criminal Law, Criminal Procedure, Evidence, and Constitutional Law. With that in mind, let's now move on to my last outline: Constitutional Law.

Constitutional Law Outline

This general outline for Constitutional Law is a bit longer than those for the other subjects I have covered in this book. Constitutional Law is extremely important because it covers the body of law derived from the interpretation and meaning of the United States Constitution. Thus, I felt that a bit more thorough outline would help you to understand all the important facets of this law school class.

I. Powers of the Federal Government: The Separation of Powers

A. Article I: The Legislative Branch

1. Main Powers Given to Congress

   a. Interstate Commerce: Congress has the power to regulate interstate as well as foreign commerce.

      1.) Tenth Amendment in the Bill of Rights states that all powers not specifically designated by the Constitution is delegated to the states.

      2.) The Supreme Court has held that the power to regulate interstate commerce, granted by Congress by the Commerce Clause of the Constitution, includes the power to regulate navigation [*Gibbons v. Ogden, 22 U.S. 1, (1824)*]

Get out!
New York gave me
the <u>exclusive</u> right to
operate steamships in
New York waters.

Wrong.
New York gave
the United States
the <u>exclusive</u> right to
regulate interstate
commerce.

stus.com

b. Taxing and Spending

    1.) Limits on taxing power

        a.) Direct taxes

        b.) Customs duties and excise taxes must be uniform

        c.) No export taxes

    2.) States

        a.) Fourteenth Amendment Due Process Clause:

        Benefits and protection must have sufficient relationship to the subject taxed.

        b.) Income tax

        c.) Sales and use tax

        d.) *Ad valorem* property taxes:

        Taxes levied on real or personal property by local government, i.e., counties, municipalities, school districts, and special taxing districts.

c. Federal Property:
Congress has power to regulate and dispose of
federal property.

d. War and Defense:
Congress can declare war and can establish and
fund the armed forces.

e. Enforcement of Civil War Amendments:

1.) Congressional enforcement of civil rights

    a.) The Thirteenth Amendment abolishes
    slavery and involuntary servitude.

    b.) The Fourteenth Amendment requires
    the states to give Due Process,
    Equal Protection, and privileges and
    immunities.

    c.) The Fifteenth Amendment bars the
    states from denying voting rights on the
    basis of race, color, or previous condition
    of servitude.

2.) The power of Congress to reach private
conduct

    a.) When Congress enforces the Fourteenth
    and Fifteenth Amendments, it has some
    power to reach private conduct, but this
    power is not unlimited.

        1.] The Fourteenth and Fifteenth
        Amendments are limited to
        governmental action.

    b.) The Thirteenth Amendment is not

explicitly limited to government action, so Congress can reach certain private conduct that it can't reach through the Fourteenth and Fifteenth Amendments.

2. Shared Power: Dormant Commerce Clause

   a. Courts balance the interest of the states in regulating local matters with federal interest in creating uniformity.

   b. Cooley Doctrine:
   The principle that Congress has exclusive power under the commerce clause to regulate national commercial matters and that the states share this power, in the absence of federal preemption, with respect to local matters [*Cooley v. Board of Wardens*, 53 U.S. 299 (1852)].

3. Speech and Debate Clause:
   Special immunity for legislators and aides in specific acts.

4. Necessary and Proper Clause:
   Authority of Congress to implement enumerated powers.

   a. Exercise of implied powers is subordinate to those rights specified by the Constitution

   b. *McCulloch v. Maryland*, 17 U.S. 316 (1819); Mere rationality test applied.

      1.) First, the government must be pursuing a legitimate governmental objective.

    2.) Second, there must be a "minimally rational relation" between the means chosen by the government and the state objective.

B. Article II: The Executive Branch

1. Presidential Powers:

   These are generally broader in the foreign arena than in domestic affairs.

   a. Main powers of the President:

      1.) Execution of Laws:

         The President executes and carries out the laws made by Congress.

      2.) Commander in Chief:

         The President directs and leads our armed forces, but cannot declare war. Only Congress can do this.

      3.) Treaty and Foreign Affairs:

         The President can make treaties with foreign nations, but only if two-thirds of the Senate approves.

      4.) Appointment of Federal Officers:

         The President appoints all federal officers, including cabinet members, federal judges, and ambassadors. The Senate must approve all such federal officers by majority vote.

         a.) Inferior federal officers and employees

            1.] Congress decides whether they should be appointed by the President, judicial branch, or "heads of departments" (i.e., cabinet members). Congress can only decide who can make these appointments; they cannot make these lower-level appointments themselves.

5.) Pardons:

The President can issue pardons for federal crimes only.

    a.) President can't pardon anyone who has been impeached and convicted.

    b.) A full pardon restores innocence and all civil rights.

6.) Veto:

The President may veto any law passed by both houses, but can be overridden by a two-thirds majority of each house.

    a.) One-house veto is unconstitutional [*Ins v. Chadha*, 462 U.S. 919 (1983)].

2. Impeachment:

  a. Impeachment of President

    1.) House: Majority to invoke changes

    2.) Senate: Two-thirds to convict

    3.) Grounds: Treason, bribery, high crimes, and misdemeanors.

  b. Impeachment of Federal Office:

Congress has sole power

  c. Criminal Liability

        1.) In addition to impeachment and does *not* constitute double jeopardy.

   3. Immunity

     a. Civil Liability

        1.) Absolute immunity of President with regard to official acts but not unofficial conduct. Also applies to testimony of grand jury witnesses and trial witnesses.

        2.) Qualified immunity of all government officials, unless actions violate clearly established law.

     b. Executive Privilege:
Qualified privilege with regard to disclosure of confidential information.

C. Article III: The Judiciary

   1. The Nature and Source of the Supreme Court's Authority

     a. Review of congressional acts, state laws, and state court judgments

        1.) Standards of Review

           a.) Strict scrutiny

              1.] Requirements: *compelling objective* & *necessary means*

              2.] Applied by the Court in the following contexts:

                  a.] Substantive due process/ fundamental rights

                  b.] Equal Protection if the

classification relates to either
a suspect classification or
fundamental right

c.] Freedom of expression

d.] Freedom of religion/free exercise
clause

b.) Mere rationality

1.] Requirements:

Easiest to satisfy by legitimate state
objective and rational relation.

2.] Is applied by the Court mainly in the
following instances:

a.] Dormant Commerce Clause

b.] Substantive due process, so
long as no fundamental right is
affected.

c.] Equal Protection:

The Court uses this level of
review so long as no suspect,
semi-suspect classification,
or fundamental rights being
impaired

d.] Contracts Clause:

Applies to some aspects of the
"obligations of contracts" clause.

c.) Middle level review

1.] Requirements:

Must have important objective and
substantially related means.

2.] Used by the Court in a small number of contexts:

    a.] Equal Protection/quasi-suspect: gender and illegitimacy.

    b.] Contracts Clause applies to conduct attacked under "Obligation of Contracts" Clause.

    c.] Free expression/non-content based (e.g., any content-neutral "time, place, and manner" regulation).

  b. The Supreme Court reviews the constitutionality of executive and legislative branch acts.

    1.) The ultimate power to interpret the Constitution is determined by the Supreme Court [*Marbury v. Madison*, 5 U.S. 137 (1803)].

2. Congress' Authority to Limit Federal Court Jurisdiction

  a. The Constitution specifically prescribes the Supreme Court's original jurisdiction involving cases affecting states and ambassadors

    1.) Congress may not add to or take away from that jurisdiction.

      a.) However, the Supreme Court exercises its appellate jurisdiction at Congress' discretion.

1.] Appeal of right:
Supreme Court is obligated to hear
the matter.

2.] Certiorari:
Discretionary appeal granted by four
votes.

3. Article VI: Supremacy Clause:
State courts must follow federal law, which is the
supreme law of the land.

4. The federal judiciary may decide "cases" or
"controversies" that fall within the federal judicial
power.

   a. Case or Controversy Requirement

      1.) Justiciability:
Types of matters that the federal courts can
adjudicate; in order for a case to be
heard by federal courts, the plaintiff must
get past these procedural obstacles which are
referred to as *requirements for justiciability*.

         a.) Nonjusticiable

            1.] Political questions

            2.] Advisory opinions and hypothetical
or abstract issues.

         b.) Standing:
A personal stake in the outcome.

            1.] Specific injury-in-fact

            2.] Remedy or relief must be available.

            3.] Third party standing (*jus tertii*):

          Sometimes granted to a party claiming to protect the rights or interests of a third party.

    c.) Ripeness ("too soon")

       1.] Real or immediate threat of harm must exist.

    d.) Mootness ("too late")

       1.] Controversy must exist at all stages of the lawsuit.

       2.] Exceptions:

         a.] Capable of repetition, yet evading review;

         b.] Voluntary cessation by defendant;

         c.] Collateral consequences.

5. The Eleventh Amendment and Suits Against the States

The Eleventh Amendment states that:

The Judicial power of the United States shall not be construed to extend to any suit in law or equity, commenced or prosecuted against one of the United States by Citizens of another State, or by Citizens or Subjects of any Foreign State.

    a. Applies to damage suits against states, but *not* injunctions

    b. Does *not* bar federal suits brought by one state against another state, or by the federal government against a state

    c. *Only* the state itself, not its counties or cities, is

protected by the Eleventh Amendment

d. Congress cannot override the Eleventh Amendment

6. States' Sovereign Immunity

   a. The states have constitutional sovereign immunity from private damage suits brought against the state in the state's own courts

   b. The states also have sovereign immunity from being required to respond to a private complaint before a federal administrative agency.

II. The Due Process Clause of the Fourteenth Amendment
A. Overview:

1. The individual rights conferred by the Constitution protect only against government action, and not against acts by private individuals.

   a. Exception: The Thirteenth Amendment's ban on slavery applies to private conduct.

2. The Bill of Rights does not directly apply to states, but the Fourteenth Amendment (which does apply to states) has been interpreted to make nearly all the Bill of Rights guarantees applicable to states.

   a. The only Bill of Rights guarantees not incorporated are:

      1.) Grand Jury:
         The Fifth Amendment right not to be subject to a criminal trial without a grand jury indictment.

      2.) Right to Jury in Civil Cases:

Seventh Amendment right to jury in civil cases does not apply to states.

3.) Excessive Fines:

Eighth Amendment prohibition on excessive fines does not apply to states but the excessive bail prohibition does apply to states.

3. Rights contained in the Due Process Clause
   a. The right to due process (assurance that all legal proceedings will be fair and reasonable)
   b. The right to Equal Protection
   c. The right to the privileges or immunities of national citizenship

4. Difference between the Fifth Amendment's Due Process Clause and the Due Process Clause contained in the Fourteenth Amendment.
   a. Fifth Amendment Due Process Clause: Applies to regulations imposed by the federal government.
   b. Fourteenth Amendment Due Process Clause: Applies to regulations done by a state or local government.

B. Substantive Due Process:

Limits the substantive power of the states to regulate certain areas of human life.

1. Economic and social regulation
   a. If the right does not fall within the grouping of "fundamental rights," the state must merely act

rationally in pursuit of some health, safety or other "general welfare" goal.

2. Protection of fundamental rights
   a. If a state or federal regulation is impairing a fundamental right, the Court strictly scrutinizes the regulation.
      1.) The objective being pursued by the state must be *compelling* and
      2.) The means chosen by the state must be *necessary* to achieve that compelling end.
   b. Fundamental rights for the purpose of substantive due process include sex, marriage, and children issues
      1.) Right to Privacy
         a.) Marriage:
            Both opposite-sex and same-sex.
         b.) Child-bearing
            1.] Abortion
               a.] As a result of the two most important post-*Roe v. Wade* abortion cases [*Whole Woman's Health v. Hellerstedt*, 579 U.S. ___ (2016), and *Planned Parenthood of Southeastern Pennsylvania v. Casey*, 505 U.S. 833 (1992)], the state can regulate the abortion process so long as the state follows these principles:

       i. The regulation pursues a legitimate state interest; and

      ii. The regulation does not place an "undue burden" on the woman's right to obtain an abortion before the fetus has attained *viability* (the ability to survive outside the womb).

  c.) Child-rearing

  d.) Contraception

  c. Generally, most substantive issues are reviewed under Equal Protection grounds.

C. Procedural Due Process:

Requirement under the Fourteenth Amendments Due Process Clause that the state act with adequate or fair procedures when it deprives a person of life, liberty, or property.

1. Two main questions:

  a. Has the individual's life, liberty, or property been taken?

  b. If so, what process was "due" to him prior to the taking?

2. Limited to guarantees of fair decision-making process:

  a. Individuals are entitled to a fair procedure (hearing) before being deprived of a life, liberty, or property interest.

b. *Mathews v. Eldridge*, 424 U.S. 319 (1976), balancing test:
Private interest affected and risk of erroneous deprivation v. government's interest.

3. Liberty:
Significant governmental restraints on physical freedom, exercise of fundamental rights, and freedom of choice or action require a procedural safeguard.

4. Property:
The government cannot take "property" without procedural due process.

   a. Conventional property:
   Personal and real property.

   b. Government benefits

   1.) If a person has already been getting the benefits, the government cannot terminate those benefits without procedural due process.

   2.) However, if the state statute governing welfare benefits says that "benefits may be cut off at any time," the person has no claim to due process.

   c. Government employment

   1.) Applicant has no property interest and thus, no right to due process.

   2.) Already employed, state law applies:

   a.) Ordinarily a job is terminable at will, so

jobholder has no property right to it and may be fired without due process.

b.) If a statute or public employer's practices give employee a legitimate claim of entitlement to keep job, this is a property interest requiring due process.

D. Equal Protection

1. Overview

   a. The Equal Protection Clause is part of the Fourteenth Amendment and guarantees that people who are similarly situated will be treated similarly.

   b. Applies to both state and federal government.

   c. The Equal Protection Clause and the Fifth Amendment's Due Process Clause apply only to government action (state action), not to actions of private citizens.

      1.) Private parties outside of government do not have to comply with the procedural or substantive due process under the Fourteenth Amendment, unless either of the doctrines below apply:

         a.) Public function doctrine: Under 42 USCS § 1983 (civil action for deprivation of rights), a private person's actions constitute state action if the private person performs functions that are traditionally reserved to the state.

      b.) State involvement doctrine:
        Even if the private individual is not
        doing something that's traditionally
        a "public function," his conduct may
        constitute state action if the state is
        heavily involved in his activities.

        1.] Licensing: The fact that the state has
           licensed a private person is generally
           not enough to convert the private
           person's conduct into state action
           [*Moose Lodge v. Irvis*, 407 U.S. 163,
           (1972)].

2. Nature of Classifications
  a. Suspect classifications
    1.) Race
    2.) National origin
    3.) Alienage (can also be a quasi-suspect class)
  b. Quasi-suspect classes
    1.) Gender
    2.) Illegitimacy
    3.) Alienage (can also be a suspect class)
  c. Non-suspect classes
    1.) Age
    2.) Wealth
    3.) Mental illness or mental retardation
    4.) Sexual orientation

3. Fundamental rights whenever a classification
burdens a fundamental right or fundamental
interest:

a. In Due Process, the fundamental rights are ones related to privacy.

b. In Equal Protection, the fundamental rights are related to a variety of other interests protected by the Constitution.

    1.) Short list of rights that are fundamental for Equal Protection:

        a.) The right to marry (even for same-sex couples);

        b.) The right to vote;

        c.) The right to have access to the courts for certain kinds of proceedings; and

        d.) The right to migrate interstate:

            1.] The right to travel.

            2.] The right to change one's state of residence or employment.

4. Three Levels of Review

a. Ordinary mere rationality review: Easiest-to-satisfy standard of review.

    1.) Applies to statutes that

        a.) are not based on a suspect classification;

        b.) do not involve a quasi-suspect category (mainly gender and illegitimacy); and

        c.) do not impair a fundamental right.

    2.) Most economic and social-welfare legislation falls into this category.

b. Strict scrutiny

        1.) Applies to statutes which are based on a

           a.) suspect classification; or

           b.) impairs a fundamental right.

    c. Middle level review

        1.) Standard: The means chosen by the legislature (e.g., the classification) must be substantially related to an important government objective.

        2.) Mainly used for cases involving cases based on gender and illegitimacy.

III. Freedom of Expression

A. First Amendment rights regarding freedom of expression:

1. Freedom of speech;
2. Freedom of the press;
3. Freedom of assembly;
4. Freedom of petition; and
5. Freedom of association (derived from individuals' rights of speech and assembly).

B. Is government action that seems to infringe upon freedom of expression content-based or content-neutral?

1. Content-based action:
   Subject to strict scrutiny and rarely sustained, a governmental action that burdens a person's expression is content-based if the government

is aiming at the communicative impact of the expression.

2. Content-neutral action:
Subject to a much less demanding standard and more likely to be upheld.

a. The government is aiming at something other than the communicative impact of the expression, even though it may have the *effect* of burdening the expression.

C. Content-based government action

1. Unprotected categories:
If the speech falls into one of these pre-defined unprotected categories, the government can basically ban that expression completely based on its content, without any interference from the 1st Amendment.

a. Incitement
1.) Advocacy of imminent lawless behavior.
2.) Utterance of fighting words (e.g., words that are likely to start an immediate physical conflict).
b. Obscenity
c. Misleading or deceptive speech (e.g., fraud)
d. Speech integral to criminal conduct
1.) Speech that is part of a conspiracy to commit a crime or
2.) Speech proposing an illegal transaction.
e. Defamation

    1.) *New York Times v. Sullivan* Test [376 U.S. 254 (1964)]:

    Applies to public officials and public figures

    a.) Actual malice requirement

        1.] Statement was made either with *knowledge* that it was false, or with *reckless disregard* of whether it was true or false.

2. Not totally unprotected:

  Government must regulate in a viewpoint neutral way.

  a. The government can exclude certain subjects entirely, but it cannot single out certain viewpoints for less favorable treatment.

3. Protected category

  a. All expression not falling into one of the above five categories is protected, presumed to be unconstitutional, and subject to strict scrutiny standard.

    1.) The regulation will be sustained only if it:

      a.) Serves a compelling government objective; and

      b.) Is necessary (drawn as narrowly as possible to achieve the objective).

D. Content-neutral regulations

1. Three-part test to determine if a government restriction is content-neutral:

      a. Significant government interest;

      b. Narrowly tailored; and

      c. Alternative channels.

  2. Is a mid-level review for content-neutral restrictions that significantly impair expression (as opposed to strict scrutiny for content-based restrictions).

E. Overbreadth:

A law is unconstitutional or void for being too broad if it covers activities that are protected by the federal Bill of Rights or the rights listed in state constitutions.

1. Burdens more activities than necessary.

2. Prohibits or chills protected freedom of expression.

3. Standing: Overbreadth is really an exception to the usual rule of "standing."

4. In cases where the statute is aimed at conduct that has expressive content (rather than against pure speech), the overbreadth doctrine will only be applied if the overbreadth would be "substantial" (i.e., the potential unconstitutional applications of the statute must be reasonably numerous compared with the constitutional applications).

F. Vagueness:

A statute is unconstitutionally vague if the conduct forbidden by it is so unclearly defined that a reasonable person would have to guess at its meaning.

1. No clear notice of what is prohibited and no ascertainable standards.

2. Vagueness is an argument typically used in criminal cases (occasionally covers civil matters as well).

3. Distinguish vagueness from overbreadth:
They both leave the citizen uncertain about which applications of a statute may constitutionally be imposed. But in overbreadth, the uncertainty is hidden or "latent," and in vagueness the uncertainty is easily apparent.

G. Time, place, and manner regulations

1. Three-part test:
   a. Content neutral
   b. Narrowly tailored for significant governmental interest
   c. Alternative channels

2. Although the government cannot regulate the contents of a speech, it can place reasonable time, place, and manner restrictions on speech for the public safety [*Cox v. New Hampshire*, 312 U.S. 569 (1941)].
   a. Licensing:
   Governmental attempts to require a license or permit before expressive conduct takes place.
   b. Right to be left alone:
   As a general rule, it is up to the unwilling listener or viewer to avoid the undesired expression.
   c. Canvassing:
   A speaker's right to canvas also receives substantial protection.

d. Fighting words:

This is an unprotected category, and fighting words are those which are likely to make the person to whom they are addressed commit an act of violence.

   1.) Expressions that fall within the fighting words category can be flatly banned or punished by the state.

      a.) Limitations:

         1.] Anger not enough,

         2.] Crowd control; and

         3.] Dislike of speaker identity.

e. Offensive language:

Language that is offensive is nonetheless protected by the First Amendment.

   1.) Exceptions where offensive language can be punished or prohibited:

      a.) The audience is a captive one; or

      b.) The language is obscene (lewd without socially redeeming value)

f. Regulation of hate speech

g. Injunctions against expressive conduct

h. The public forum

   1.) Content-based regulations:

Strict scrutiny is applied whether or not the expression is or is not a public forum.

   2.) Neutral time, place, and manner:

Less likely to be upheld where expression takes place in a public forum.

3.) Examples of public forums:

    a.) Traditional public forums:

        Streets, sidewalks, and parks.

    b.) Designated public forums:

        Places where government meetings take place, and school classrooms after hours.

4.) Examples of non-public forums:

    Airport terminals, jails, military bases, insides of courthouses, and government workplace.

H. Regulation of symbolic expression

1. Expression that consists solely of non-verbal actions.

    a. Any attempt by the government to restrict symbolic expression due to content is subject to strict scrutiny.

    b. Any restriction on the time, place, or manner of symbolic speech will have to be narrowly tailored to a significant governmental objective and will have to leave open an alternative channel.

I. Commercial speech

1. Speech advertising a product or proposing some commercial transaction gets First Amendment protection.

2. The government may restrict truthful commercial speech only if the regulation directly advances a substantial governmental interest in a way that is

no more extensive than necessary to achieve the government's objective.

3. Mid-level review is applied to government restrictions based on the content of commercial speech.

   a. Contrast content-based regulations on non-commercial speech where strict scrutiny level of review is applied

4. False or deceptive commercial speech may be forbidden by the government, as well as speech which proposes an illegal transaction.

   a. If the product or service is harmful but lawful, the state may not limit advertising about it.

5. The overbreadth doctrine does not apply in commercial speech cases.

6. Lawyers have a limited right to advertise.

J. The media

1. Broadcast

   a. Federal Communications Commission (FCC) regulations are given deference.

   b. In general, the government will not be able to obtain a *prior restraint* against broadcasters or publishers.

      1. In First Amendment law, *prior restraint* is government action that prohibits speech or other expression before the speech happens.

   c. FCC is granted limited power to regulate indecent language.

2. The press
   a. Freedom of the press grants newspapers the right to choose what to print.
   b. Access to information is limited to that granted to the general public.
   c. Release of names of confidential sources are protected on a state-by-state basis under state shield laws.

K. **Freedom of association:**
   In general, if an individual has a First Amendment right to engage in a particular expressive activity, then a group has a "freedom of association" right to engage in that same activity as a group.
   1. Right not to associate:
      Individuals and groups also have a well-protected "right not to associate."
      a. Any government attempt to do the following will be strictly scrutinized:
         1.) Make an individual give financial support to a cause s/he dislikes; or
         2.) Make a group take members whose presence would interfere with the group's expressive activities.
   2. Illegal membership:
      The freedom of association means that mere membership in a group or association may not be made illegal.
      a. Membership in a group may only be made part of an offense if:

      1.) The group is actively engaged in unlawful activity, or incites others to imminent lawless action; and

      2.) The individual knows of the group's illegal activity, and specifically intends to further the group's illegal goals.

3. Denial of public jobs and benefits:
   Freedom of expression also prevents the government from denying a public benefit or job based on a person's association.
   a. Non-illegal activities
   b. No right/privilege
   c. Compulsory disclosure:
      The government may not force you to disclose your membership activities (or require a group to disclose who its members are), unless it could make that membership illegal.
   d. Exceptions:
      1.) Partisan political activities
      2.) Patronage hirings:
         Some public jobs may be awarded as patronage appointments, ones the performance of which is reasonably related to a person's politics.
      3.) Speech critical of superiors or otherwise inappropriate:
         An employee gets only limited protection for speech or associational activities that are critical of superiors.

    a) Where the speech involves a matter of "public concern," the Court will balance the speech rights of the employee and the government's interest as employer in promoting efficiency on the job.

    b) Where the speech does not involve a matter of public concern, the Court gives great deference to the employer's judgment.

IV. Freedom of Religion
A. Establishment Clause

1. Main purpose is to prevent government from endorsing or supporting religion.

2. *Lemon v. Kurtzman,* **403 U.S. 602** (1971) test

    a. Law must have a secular legislative purpose (known as the Purpose Prong);

    b. Law must have primary secular effect that neither advances nor inhibits religion (known as the Effect Prong); and

    c. Law must not create "excessive government entanglement" with religion (known as the Entanglement Prong).

        1.) If any of these prongs are violated, the government's action is deemed unconstitutional under the Establishment Clause of the First Amendment to the United States Constitution.

B. Free Exercise

1. Main purpose of this clause is to prevent the government from outlawing or seriously burdening a person's pursuit of whatever religion he chooses.

   a. Protects belief absolutely and conduct to a lesser degree.

C. Applicable to the states:

Both clauses only restrict legislative action by Congress. However, both clauses have been interpreted to apply also to the states, by means of the Fourteenth Amendment's Due Process Clause.

D. Conflict:

When the two clauses seem to conflict, the Free Exercise Clause dominates. If a particular benefit or accommodation to religion is arguably required by the Free Exercise Clause, then when the government grants that accommodation or benefit it is not violating the Establishment Clause.

V. Miscellaneous Clauses

A. Fourteenth Amendment Privileges and Immunities

1. National rights only

   a. Right to travel from state to state (also protected by Equal Protection Clause)

   b. Right to vote in national elections

2. Right to change state of residence

3. Strict scrutiny standard applied by the Court to state laws that interfere with the rights of national citizenship [*Saenz v. Roe*, 526 U.S. 489 (1999)]

B. Takings Clause of Fifth Amendment

1. The Fifth Amendment to the United States Constitution places an important limitation on the power of eminent domain. It says, in part, "… nor shall private property be taken for public use, without just compensation."

   a. Contrast this to police power, coming from the Tenth Amendment, which is the state's inherent right to regulate an individual's conduct or property to protect the health, safety, welfare, and morals of the community. Unlike the exercise of eminent domain, no compensation need be paid.

2. Although protection under the Takings Clause originally applied only to takings of property by the federal government, the Fourteenth Amendment later extended this protection to takings by the states and their political subdivisions.

3. Two types of governmental appropriations of property ('takings'):

   a. Direct condemnation involves the exercise of eminent domain powers.

   b. With inverse condemnation, the government takes property from an individual, but denies that it is using its power of eminent domain and does not pay.

      1.) There are three types of "taking by inverse condemnation":

a.) Permanent physical occupation:
When the government is permanently
occupying someone else's property.
1.] Per se taking;
2.] A temporary physical occupation,
however, is not a per se taking.
b.) Land-use exaction:
Compensation that a development is
required to cede to the government
before constructing a new structure or
putting land to a new use; "takings"
liability can arise in certain situations
where governmental exactions are
imposed as conditions of developmental
approval.
1.] In *Nollan* [*Nollan v. California Coastal
Commission*, 483 U.S. 825 (1987)]
and *Dolan* [*Dolan v. City of Tigard*,
512 U.S. 687 (1994)], the Supreme
Court announced a two-part test for
the evaluation of exaction conditions.
a.] The government must show
there is both a "nexus" and "rough
proportionality" between the
government exaction and the
impact of the proposed land use.
b.] Applies to situations where a

governmental entity demands the conveyance of a real property interest as a condition of development approval.

2.] In *Koontz* [*Koontz v. St. Johns River Water Management District*, 568 U.S. ___ (2013)], the Supreme Court has expanded the *Nollan* and *Dolan* takings analysis to situations where:

    a.] Development approval is not granted; and

    b.] Government exaction is a payment in money.

c.) Regulatory

    1.] Regulations are generally not a taking [*Kaiser Aetna v. U.S.*, 444 U.S. 164 (1979)]

        a.] Zoning, for example, substantially interferes with property rights but isn't a taking.

        b.] The decision whether or not a taking has occurred is made by judicial consideration of three factors [three-factor Penn Central Test, *Penn Central Transportation Co. v. City of New York*, 438 U.S. 104 (1978)].

        i. The nature of the government regulation

       ii. The economic impact of the regulation on the subject property

     iii. The extent to which the regulation interferes with the owner's reasonable, investment-backed expectations

C. Contract Clause (Article I, section 10)

1. This clause provides that "no state shall…pass…law impairing the obligation of contracts."
2. Applies to both federal and state government.
3. Different levels of review for public v. private contracts.

D. The Second Amendment "Right to Bear Arms"

1. Applicable to private individuals:
   This amendment confers on private individuals a right to keep basic firearms, including handguns, at home for self-defense. [*District of Columbia v. Heller*, 554 U.S. 570, 2008)]
2. Applicable to states and cities:
   Applies the same way to state and local governments as to the federal government. [*McDonald v. City of Chicago*, 561 U.S. 742 (2010)]

E. *Ex Post Facto* laws

1. Article I prohibits both states and federal

governments from passing any "ex facto" law.

    a. An *ex post facto* law is a law which has a retroactive punitive effect.

    b. *Ex post facto* laws apply only to measures that are criminal or penal, not to those that are civil.

F. Bills of Attainder

1. Article I also prohibits both the federal government and states from passing any "bill of attainder"

2. A bill of attainder is a legislative act which applies either to named individuals or to easily ascertainable members of a group in such a way as to punish them without a judicial trial.

Extra credit:

This class was packed with numerous detailed rules and cases that we studied. When I quizzed myself using my general outline to prepare for finals, I would try to add these particular nuances.

On a Constitutional Law exam, any time you have a test question in which Congress is doing something, first ask yourself, "Can what Congress is doing be justified as an exercise of the Commerce power?" Most of the time, the answer will be yes. Another fact pattern you may have on your Constitutional Law exam might involve a state or federal government taking away something of value that could be considered "life", "liberty", or "property". One of the issues would be whether the government used proper procedures, and another issue would be whether the government, by carrying out this taking, violated the individual's substantive interest in life, liberty, or property (You would then do a Fourteenth Amendment Due Process and Substantive Due Process analysis).

Yet another likely exam topic might involve race-conscious affirmative action. Your professor may have a question on the exam in which the government is trying to help racial or ethnic minorities by giving them some sort of preference. The issues you should be focusing on in such a question would be Equal Protection and the strict scrutiny standard.

Throughout this and the other outlines in this book, I have added some important current cases that have come into play since I was in law school in the 1980s. For instance, in terms of the special immunity for legislators and aides in official acts under the Speech and Debate Clause of the U.S. Constitution, the Supreme Court held in 1998 that absolute immunity from civil liability extends to federal, state, regional and local legislators [*Bogan v. Scott-Harris*, 523 US 44 (1998)]. The law has also evolved with cases regarding government takings of property, the Fourteenth Amendment Privileges and Immunities Clause, the Second Amendment Right to Bear Arms, freedom of speech, and abortion rights. I have updated this outline to reflect these changes as well.

INDEX

About the Author

TERESA POWER, JD, is an internationally recognized educator, yoga expert, and author of *The ABCs of Law School: Diary of a First Year Student* and the bestselling series, *The ABCs of Yoga for Kids®*.

Her multiple award-winning books and learning tools have been translated into four languages. Teresa's workshops and keynotes have been attended by tens of thousands at numerous conferences, schools, bookstores, and other venues across the United States.

She has appeared on both local and national television and radio and has been featured in/on Good Morning America, CBS Los Angeles, Telemundo Los Angeles, Fox News Los Angeles, *Reader's Digest*, *Publishers Weekly*, *Foreword Magazine*, Sirius XM, *USA Today Magazine*, *Girls World* Magazine, *Yoga Digest*, Glamour.com, Parenting.com and more. Teresa was also named a KNX-AM "Hero of the Week" in 2017, honoring her dedication to helping yoga become accessible to children all over the world.

Teresa enjoys volunteering her time with the University of Southern California, Let's Move West LA, SOS Mentor, the Boys and Girls Clubs of America, Children's Bureau, Connections for Children, Pathways, and Choose Health LA Child Care. She also has a monthly column in the *Palisadian Post* newspaper called "The Pose".

A graduate of University of Southern California, she earned her JD from Pepperdine University School of Law and completed a yoga training program with Indigo Yoga.

For more information, please visit Teresa's website at www.abclawschooldiary.com. Teresa is available for workshops, speaking engagements, and instruction.

BONUS CONTENT

TO ACCESS THE BONUS CONTENT featured in *The ABCs of Law School: Diary of a First Year Student*, visit www.abclawschooldiary.com, click on "Downloads" and enter code 33627.

5-Minute-a-Day Yoga Routine

Practice these 12 poses for just 5 minutes a day to become calm, fit, and flexible. Practicing simple yoga postures is the ideal way to naturally unwind and obtain physical activity at the same time. There is no need to have a yoga mat; a beach towel or carpet is sufficient. You can flow from one pose to the next, holding each posture for around 20 seconds before moving on. Remember to breathe in and out through your nose while focusing on the breath. End with Corpse Pose; close your eyes and stay still for at least 60 seconds to gain all the benefits of the previous postures.

1. Child's Pose
2. Cat/Cow Pose
3. Downward Facing Dog Pose
4. Chair Pose
5. Warrior Pose
6. Tree Pose
7. Cobra Pose
8. Bow Pose
9. Reclining Pigeon Pose
10. Bridge Pose
11. Seated Twisted Poses
12. Corpse Pose

For instructions on how to do the poses, refer to Chapter 14, page 165.

© 2019 Teresa Power
Illustrations by Ivana Mundja